The Image
In The Mirror II

Manifesting A Dream Deferred

A Heart of Love! pg 140.
My story is about restoration
after trauma. Finding Joy, Peace,
keeping the faith after a storm.
Love, Restoration, Forgiveness, Joy

Thank you.

Compiled by:

VISIONARY AUTHOR

JOAN T RANDALL

5/29/22

Published by Victorious You Press™

Unless otherwise indicated, scripture quotations are from the Holy Bible, New King James Version. All rights reserved.

Printed in the United States of America

ISBN: 978-1-952756-60-3

For details, email joan@victoriousy-
oupress.com
or visit us at www.victoriousyoupress.com

DEDICATION

To the woman who has had the most profound impact and influence on my life, my beloved mom, Ena Rebecca Hibbert-Thaxter.

Who I am and what I do today directly reflect her legacy.

ACKNOWLEDGEMENT

To the Authors of this book-you are the most accurate definition of resilience, perseverance, forgiveness, grace, and truth. Thank you for going on this ride with me and trusting me to tell your stories in print and film. I am humbled.

Rev. Allison Daniels, Shania Elliott-McDowell, Pastor Charles Kearse, Vern Hamil, Amy Hayes, Tonya Barbee, Tamra T. Bush, Patty Lauterjung, Trina San, Nadia Monsano, Angela Mitchell, Tamika McTier, Permethia Rudy Milton, Jacqueline Sinclair, Donna Murrell, and Donna Thompson thank you for being the examples as you poured your hearts out for the world to read.

To my Editor, Lynn Braxton, thank you for the excellence in which you executed your editing craft and brought the stories in this book to life.

To my Documentary Director, Erika Etienne, your vision for the flow of the stories was brilliant.

The manner and depth at which you pulled the stories from the authors for the film was truly fascinating. You ensured the camera lens captured the beauty of each author's manifestation of their dream deferred. You are indeed exceptional.

To my Graphic Designer, Nadia Monsano, thank you for sharing your gift with me and the world. Your creativity and attention to detail is showcased in the book cover and all the marketing promotional materials.

To my Husband, Bill, thank you for your love and patience while I was working on this project.

To my sister Shelly-Ann Sylver, you are my balance and my rock. God knew I needed a twin when he created you.

To my children-Kay, Shay, Brianna, and Brandon. Thank you for giving me the space and the grace to walk in my calling.

Last but not least, to my beautiful grandchildren, my forever loves. My heart beats differently for you guys. My love is fierce, yet gentle, and you all have my heart wrapped up around you: Maicol, Gabriel, Raegan, Ena Sofia, and Izzy. This is your legacy.

TABLE OF CONTENTS

INTRODUCTION

A Dream Deferred does not have to be a Dream Denied

Ena Rebecca

Ena Rebecca was born in rural St. Elizabeth on the Island of Jamaica during the 1930s and was her mother's second child of four children. She never knew her father when she was growing up. Life for her family was hard and resources were relatively meager. Their source of livelihood was dependent on farming and livestock, and every child had to help with the day-to-day tasks. Nevertheless, Ena was brilliant and loved going to school. It was an escape each day from the hard life she experienced. Her favorite subjects were European history and geography. Her dreams were to become a teacher. She knew that would change the trajectory of her life as she thought about her future. She was young and naïve, but her innocence was unwillingly and brutally snatched from her at the tender age of four-teen by someone who was twice her age. And at fifteen, she found herself giving birth to a baby boy. Only a child herself, the shame and scrutiny were enough to crush her spirit and self-esteem and shatter her dreams.

There were no repercussions for what was done to her, and she had to live with the fact that school and her education were no longer an option. As a teenage mother of a child with an absentee

1

father, she had to do what she could to take care of her baby. She wrestled with her circumstances and the fate of her life and adjusted to a dream now shelved. Still, she kept learning on her own. Whatever history books she could get her hands on, she would immerse herself in them and absorb the information. Reading and history became Ena's hobbies.

Years passed, Ena married and welcomed three children with her husband, Rudolph. Although her dreams of becoming a teacher were far gone, she taught her three children everything she knew about European history and encouraged them to read daily. She pushed them to be the best students possible as she knew that education was the key out of poverty.

She died not being able to manifest her dreams, but today, her children are living out their dreams due to her sacrifice and legacy. **Ena was my mother.**

Rudolph Slater

Rudolph, my dad, had a voice like an angel. It was his divine gift from the Holy Spirit. He would sing to everyone who would listen. I grew up listening to him belt out tunes, the likes of Nat King Cole, Engelbert Humperdinck, Perry Como, Steve Lawrence, and his voice was just as flawless. My dad grew up in an era in Jamaica when education was not the priority; instead, a male child was expected to get a job and work as soon as they were fourteen. And that is what he did. There was no going after your dreams and goals—that was not what he saw growing up. His parents worked hard to keep a roof over the family's head and their parents before them, so that was all my dad knew to do. His essence was love and singing to his children. That was what he gave us because it was the only way he knew how to.

Rudolph was talented in many ways. He had exceptional abilities and mastered plumbing and carpentry like his father before him. So, he got caught up in the race of just surviving to make ends meet for his family.

Although his lifelong dream was to become a singer, he never understood how to use the beautiful gift of his voice to make his dream of becoming a star a reality. Unfortunately, lack of knowledge and limited resources deterred and deferred his dreams.

When Rudolph left this earth, his dreams were buried with him.

Beverley Minerva

She was tall, elegant, had curly brown hair, and looked like a movie star. The first time I remembered genuinely taking notice of her, I was about four years old, and she left an indelible impression on me. She only wore stilettos and always polished her nails in red. Her red lipstick would be evident on the cigarette as she held it between the index and middle fingers of her right hand. When she inhaled the cigarette, she would blow the smoke out on the right side of her mouth. She was my Aunty Minnie and my personal celebrity.

I loved when Aunty came to visit my parents. She was my dad's baby sister, and they were extremely close. As soon as she arrived, I would take her handbag and put it over my shoulder. Once she took off her shoes, I put my tiny feet into those four-inch stilettos—that's where I got my training to walk in high heels.

Aunty Minnie, as she is affectionally called, is a plant whisperer. She has a green thumb and speaks to her flowers. It always marveled me how they would respond. If she were tending to a plant that was not blossoming or blooming well, she would have a conversation with them, and the next day they would look better. Her dream was to become a Horticulturalist.

3

She was fortunate enough to work for the College of Agriculture in Portland, Jamaica, and had access to all the educational resources and expert training to launch her nursery. She also owned the land on which she could have established her nursery. Instead, however, she placed her incredible gift on the back shelf, and year, after year, after year, she deferred her dreams.

A few weeks ago, I visited my Aunty Minnie in a hospital in Florida as she had suffered a heart attack and now has three blocked arteries. At eighty-one years old, she refused the triple bypass open-heart surgery needed to repair the damage from fifty-plus years of smoking. During our heart-to-heart conversation, she told me that her biggest regret in life was putting her dreams on hold and never activating the gift that God gave her. It broke my heart.

****

My motivation for this book was inspired by the people I love the most. Because I did not see it in my family, breaking the cycle of comfort and familiarity was one way of changing the narrative for my life and the life of my children. It was essential to show them something different from what I witnessed and experienced. But this is not just about me. I wanted to inspire others to do the same.

- Gifts, talents, and the innate ability to produce as God would have us to do are most often deferred due to insecurities, inadequacies, lack of knowledge, comfort, fear, and doubts.

- Dreams are sometimes deferred at the cost of helping others realize theirs.

- One's happiness is deferred to make someone else happy.

- Identities are sometimes lost to please others, and therefore, the dreams fade.

- Desires, joy, and peace are deferred to approve and settle into the comfort of someone else's ordinary.

There are times when dreams are deferred to the point of no return. I call this a *life on pause*—living to exist instead of living on purpose, and our hearts are never satisfied. Then, of course, there is always the yearning for more, but we disobey the command God gave us for various reasons. And at the end of our lives, some will find themselves lying on a bed before transitioning to the afterlife—regretting a dream that's gone. It is here that the *life on pause* stares them in the face with pity, and hearts are left with sadness and regret because that which they were born to do was never done. The gifts, talents, and treasures were never actualized for the purpose of kingdom building.

I hope you can see yourself in one of the stories in this book. If you find yourself thinking about that goal, that dream, that desire, that change, and feeling guilty about putting it off, I give you full permission to pull it off the shelf, dust it off, and get to it. Let me remind you of the dominion, authority, and the power you have within to achieve anything. You are already equipped with everything you need to make it happen. God Bless You!

****

If you find yourself overwhelmed or depressed, please speak to someone or seek help. You are a precious gift. Know that with God, there is nothing that you can't get through, absolutely nothing.

Peace, Love, and Light

Joan T Randall

www.victoriousyoupress.com

SECTION 1

RELENTLESS RESILIENCE

I am reminded of a seed that is buried in darkness for weeks, months, and sometimes years, where worms and other insects share the same space. But the seed stays focused, intending to build structure and strength behind the scenes to support its growth, even in that environment. It figures out a way to nourish and sustain itself, and when the time is just right, it comes forth with relentless

resilience.

"Finally, be strong in the Lord and in His mighty power."

Ephesians 6:10 New International Version

STRUGGLING TO SURVIVE

ANGELA M MITCHELL

My story is that of many women. So many mothers, daughters, sisters, etc., have experienced the trauma of sexual abuse, domestic violence, and abandonment. The effects cut so deep that it sends them down the rabbit hole of depression, anxiety, or other mental health or mood disorders. We use the term depressed loosely when we are sad about something or when things aren't going our way. We trivialize the word so people don't grasp the true seriousness of the disorder. I did this for most of my life because I never believed that it was a real issue. I certainly didn't think that I would be affected by it, that's how I ended up in a cycle of depression and anxiety. The feelings of self-doubt, insecurity, and self-hate left me convinced that I was the victim, one that will never break free, one that will never reach my fullest God-given potential. I didn't recognize back then that being victimized doesn't make you a victim. Feeling unloved and unwanted will have you looking for love in all the wrong places, from all the wrong people. That's when the darkness creeps in; that's when you feel trapped.

The last time I gave you a glimpse of who I am and where I started, I told you that I needed a hero. This time I'm going to tell you how those struggles affected the woman I became, the woman who is here right now. The woman who is leading other women to greatness. Who would have known I would make it this far when I couldn't even see myself for who I am for the longest time? I was so busy holding on to who and what I used to be that I couldn't focus on my present, so I blocked every blessing waiting for me–but the Most High saw me. When I realized that, I was able to remember who and whose I am. What I had was an awakening, more than a simple epiphany; I had a transformation. It was only then that I was able to look in the mirror without being afraid or hating what I saw. I will tell you this; once I did, I saw a woman ready to rise and take back what was stolen. I was prepared to go after my dreams that had been deferred for so long. I was a Phoenix rising from the ashes! So, take this walk with me one more time...

Dreaming

Looking back, I can honestly say that I've always been a big dreamer. On any given day you would find me lost in my thoughts and mapping out my dream life. I would daydream about getting married, having a career as a lawyer, writer, teacher, and even becoming a mother one day. I would also dream about having a father so that I could experience the love that only a father can give his daughter; every little girl needs a daddy, right? She needs her father to show her how she is supposed to be loved and treated, and he is her example of what she should expect from the men in her life. I was no different. I wanted to be a daddy's girl so badly when I was a kid. Hell, I still do. I longed for the love that only a father can give and I was going to get it one way or another. Eventually, I would get the love I was looking for (at least that's what I thought I was doing) from the boys and eventually the men that I so freely gave myself to.

I lost my virginity to a boy when I was just thirteen years old. We had been talking on the phone for a couple of weeks before we saw each other in person, so I figured that I knew him pretty well. It was a muggy, early summer morning, and my mother had gone to work. She left around five am, so the coast was clear, and I invited him over.

He got there around six, and we went straight to my room and got right to business. Now, I didn't have the slightest clue what to do, I just thought that since I liked him and he said he liked me, I was supposed to have sex with him. I think we talked for a few minutes before we started making out. I expected fireworks and rainbows, but that was not the case at all. It hurt like hell and was not enjoyable, but I let him keep going anyway because I didn't want him to think that I was a kid or that I didn't like him.

After that, I thought we were in love and would be together forever; how silly of me, I was thirteen, after all. We had sex a few more times after that, and I figured I was a woman and my mother couldn't tell me what to do anymore. I even ran away and went to his house because I thought we would live together in his mother's basement. That didn't work out, and he dumped me not long after he got what he wanted out of me. From then on, I would have sex with various boys because I thought it was the way to get them to like me. This is all before the age of fourteen years old! See, this happens when a little girl doesn't have a father to guide her and show her unconditional love. I figured if I shopped around enough that I would find what I was looking for. I was wrong, though, and it took me nearly my entire twenties and thirties to figure that out.

I walked around every day, strolling to my song with those dreams in my heart. I even had things all worked out in my head. Those things were not to be, though. Once I had my son in high school, I just never thought about taking action to make those dreams come true. I didn't understand how strong I was, so I didn't move.

I got pregnant for the first time at fourteen years old. I remember trying to hide it from my mother, but of course she figured it out. I ended up having to get rid of the baby, my first son. I was so far along that I had to deliver him once the doctor did whatever he did to end his life. I was devastated, but I kept my feelings to myself and moved on as if nothing happened. I became pregnant again at fifteen and wasn't allowed to keep that baby either, nor did I ever talk about it. I just pushed it all inward and allowed it to fester for many years.

I had my first child at seventeen and graduated from high school a month later. I moved out of my mother's house a few months later and was pregnant with my daughter soon after. I thought I was living at least one of those dreams of mine, the one where I was a wife and mother, except I didn't have the ring. But I was okay with that, and I could wait for a little while. Well, I kept waiting for that part to happen, but it would be a long and pointless wait. In the meantime, I had since given up on being anything more than what I was, which was a young mother with two kids living on welfare.

As far as I was concerned, there was nothing I could do, I didn't think I would be capable of working and going to school and raising kids. I didn't have the strength at that time, what little mental and emotional energy I had was reserved for my babies. They were my light and my hope. They're the only reason I didn't just end my life back then. I was a kid without a clue. I clung to the wrong people and took their bad advice. and I allowed myself to be misled, all because I wanted a family and someone to love me.

I was caught, no, I was trapped in the darkness of shame and regret that would hold on to me for many years and lead me to bouts of anxiety and depression. I couldn't escape because I was in a fog; my life felt like a movie that I hadn't seen in a long time and had forgotten. The truth is that I hadn't even identified or acknowledged my pain. I had to keep a brave front and stay strong for my kids. I realize now that you can't address and heal what you don't recognize.

The Struggle is Real

Damn, I can't believe I don't have anything for my babies to eat. I don't have any more food, no food stamps, no money, no nothing, I thought to myself. The first of the month was still a week away, and I had no idea what my next step would be. I looked in the cabinet and sighed loudly as I used the last two boxes of jiffy mix to make pancakes for the kids. I wasn't sure what I was going to do or who I would call for help. Their father was in and out of jail, so he was not an option, but I probably wouldn't have asked him anyway. I wouldn't ask my mother because Lord knows I didn't want to listen to the barrage of questions and the judgmental tone about why their father wasn't helping me. And I was way too embarrassed to ask any of the dudes I was messing with.

I ended up calling up my grandfather in Detroit to see if he could send me a few dollars to get some groceries to hold me over until I got my benefits the following week. I was so embarrassed to have to ask him for money, because he knew my kids' father was in the street making money, so as far as he was concerned there was no excuse for me not to have money for food. So, instead of him sending the money to me, he asked my uncle to bring me some food. Of course, I was even more humiliated when my uncle brought the groceries to my house in the hood, which was a mess, by the way because there were a lot of days that I struggled to get out of bed, let alone clean my house up. Nobody knew that, though, and that's the way I wanted to keep it.

My dreams were slowly slipping away along with my happiness and my light. I wanted so badly to give my kids the life they deserved, but I was mentally incapable of motivating myself, and I didn't have the support I so desperately needed. I was still holding on to the lie of the fairytale I had created in my head, the one where my man

13

would take care of me and my kids, and I wouldn't have to do any-thing but cook and clean. Ridiculous, I know, but I was a kid and thought I knew it all.

I Can't Get Up

Here I was, twenty years old with two kids, no job, no money, and no hope. I would live day to day smoking weed, getting drunk, and hav-ing sex, all to escape my life and my pain. All that happened was that I caused myself more harm than good and opened myself up to more pain. My house was the go-to house, the hangout spot for my friends and some of the dudes in the neighborhood. You would often find me there with my friends partying with whoever showed up that day.

There was this one night when my kids had gone over to their grandmother's house for the weekend, and I had the place to myself. I had straightened up and taken a bath so that I could watch TV and relax for a while. My brother and his friends were coming over later to take care of some business, so I had time to chill before they got there. I was in my room watching a music video and was dancing along with the music, I think the song was, "Rump Shaker" by Wrecks-n-Effect. I was popping and shaking my thang when some-one knocked at my door. *Dang, who is that?* I thought to myself. "Who Dat?" I yelled as I looked out the window. It turned out to be the dude next door. We had talked a few times in passing, but we weren't friends, so I didn't know what in the world he wanted, but I opened the door.

"Hey, what's up? Everything okay?" I asked.

"I'm locked out. Can I use your phone to make a call?" he said.

Of course, I said yes because he was my neighbor, and he had been nothing but pleasant to me. While I was leading him to the kitchen to get the phone, the eeriest feeling came over me. I became nervous. I didn't let on, but I started to make small talk.

As he was walking behind me, he said, "I saw you dancing a little while ago."

"What? When?" I replied.

"Right before I knocked on the door, I saw you through the window."

I was still trying to play it cool even though I sensed what was about to happen. He quickly put his arms around my waist and pulled me toward him. I was too scared to resist, but I was gently trying to pull away. I knew that my brother would be there soon, so I thought he would get there in time.

Then, he put his hand around my neck and started licking my ear, his nasty, hot breath was blowing in my face. "You fine as hell. I want you to be my girl," he said as he fondled me.

Now, I began to struggle and fight against him, but he started squeezing my neck harder. "You gon' give me some of this. You knew I was looking, and you were dancing for me," he said as he ripped my pants and panties off. He pushed me down on the couch and slammed into me from behind. Minutes later, my brother and his friend were knocking on the door, but the guy had his arm around my throat so that I couldn't scream. They left when I didn't answer.

When he was done, he went toward the back of the house. I froze when he told me to come into the kitchen, because I knew if I did, he would have killed me to keep me from telling on him—I felt it deep in my soul. Before he could stop me, I ran out of the house and down the street to my friend's house. She called the police and took me to the hospital. I later found out that I wasn't his first victim, and that the house next door was a group home. I was horrified to find out he was HIV positive. I was scared to death but thank God I tested negative both times. The Most High kept me, and I didn't even know it.

I was always nervous and on edge for weeks after that happened because I thought he would come back to hurt me. I had even stayed with my friend for a while. Later on, I picked his picture from some mug shot photos detectives had shown to me. He was arrested and charged, but I couldn't do it when it came time to testifying in court. I couldn't get up there and talk about how he had violated me. I thought it was my fault anyway because he knew my house was the party house. I told myself that I should never have been dancing like that, and I should have never let him in. It didn't make it any better that I was told no one would believe me because I was running the streets sleeping with different men. This kind of violation was nothing new to me though, men had been violating me since I was a little girl, maybe around five or six years old, so I had come to expect to be abused in one way or another.

You see, I had accepted that I was a victim in my own story. I made every excuse and gave myself every reason why I had gotten what I deserved. I told myself that every vile thing that happened to me was my fault and that there was nothing that would change that. All this did was remind me that I was nothing at all, and that was all I ever would be. Soon enough, I would move on and sweep it under the rug, and I went on with my life as if it never happened. I didn't speak about it again to anyone else because I didn't want to feel any more judged or ashamed than I already did. I just let it sit there for years, festering and dragging me further down into the darkness and further away from my dreams.

It's Dark in Here

As the years went by and life brought with it many twists and turns, bumps, and bruises, I became so lost that I didn't even realize that I was letting my life pass me by. All my talent and potential were sitting dormant and wasting away. I was trying to mother my children, who had become unruly, and I wasn't very good at it anyway. I know

16

I wasn't the worst mother ever; I wasn't the best either, but I was the best one I knew how to be at that time. I was trying to work and maintain my household, and I was struggling with my mental health. My mind was so cloudy and filled with poisonous thoughts that it caused me physical illness. I had started having seizures again, I hadn't had any since I was a child. There would be times when I would lay down for a nap after work and wake up in an ambulance. I didn't know which way was up, and I didn't see any light at all. That's what depression feels like—a dark cave where you are chained and bound to a wall. You look up and see the light, but your mind tells you that you are not strong enough to break free and climb out. All of my hopes and dreams had long since slipped away from me, and all I seemed to have were dark times.

I wanted so badly to pursue my dreams and live the life I had always envisioned. But, instead, I would sit around for hours, still daydreaming, still wishing, and still regretting. That's the thing about lost dreams. When they go unfulfilled, you become depressed at the thought of what could or should have been and anxious about the time you think you are wasting.

The Image

I told ya'll before that I was at my wit's end. I was emotionally, spiritually, mentally, broken. I was on the floor crying out for a miracle, for a ladder so that I could climb out of that damn cave. That's when I heard and felt the presence of the Holy Spirit, and I finally looked at myself; I was finally able to see what I had struggled for years to see. I could see that I was never forsaken or alone. I just wasn't ready yet. I still had work to do inside, and I had to get rid of those thoughts and emotions that I was battling internally every day. Those were the ones that said I would never, could never move forward, that I was stuck. But when I did, the gates of abundance opened up and flooded my life with its goodness.

My spiritual healing and growth have been a long process, and through it all, I have learned to view myself through the eyes of My Creator. Once I did, I saw the image that would lead to my transformation, the one that would allow me to manifest my deferred dreams. This image gave me the courage to change the story of victimhood that I held on to for so long. I was finally able to release it and operate on pure faith and in the gifts that the Most High instilled in me.

Today, I am able to hold my head up as I lead other women who have experienced similar pain and trauma in their lives. I have created a safe haven for these women, and I lead them down the path to self-discovery and self-awareness. This is something that was never done for me. So, I finally became the teacher that I wanted to be. and I have finally acknowledged and addressed that I have bipolar disorder, depression, and anxiety. This time around, I know that changing the way I look at mental health, changing and ridding my mind of those limiting and negative beliefs about it, have led me here. I have been transformed and renewed by the Holy Spirit.

WHAT ABOUT ME?

NADIA MONSANO

As I stepped off the aircraft that brought me from Iraq to Texas, I literally fell to my knees. I looked up to heaven and shouted, "Thank you, God, for bringing me home safely." I got on the charter bus that took me to the auditorium where my husband was waiting for me. As the bus got closer to my destination, my heart raced, and had butterflies in my stomach. I had not seen my husband in one year because I was deployed to Iraq. My mind kept drifting back to the sleepless nights, and the feeling of fear kept washing over me. I had to remind myself that I was safe. The bus finally pulled into the parking lot and we disembarked.

As the platoon leader, I had my soldiers line up to march into the auditorium. With our heads held high, and our march as crisp as it could be, we entered the building. I looked in the crowd, and there he was, my husband. Our eyes locked, and without speaking words, we said a lot. You see, my husband and I have a bond, a special connection that no one but us could understand. We can have a whole conversation with each other just by using our eyes to express our thoughts or intentions. I could not wait to have his arms wrapped around me. Finally, my commander said the words we were all waiting to hear, "You can now join your family."

It seemed like we were in a movie as we ran towards each other, moving in slow motion. Yet, we could not reach each other fast enough. When I finally fell into my husband's embrace, he wrapped his arms around me as tightly as he could. I finally was safe. I had not felt safe in a long time. He picked me up and threw me in the air, twice. Thankfully, he caught me both times.

"Baby, welcome home," he said, tenderly gazing at me with tears in his eyes. "I have missed you so much. I love you."

Smiling, I whispered softly, "Baby, let's go home." I became choked up as tears streamed down my face.

We walked to the car, holding each other tight around the waist. Feeling secure and happy, I laid my head on his arm. The drive home was so surreal to me. I kept looking over at my husband to make sure I was not dreaming. He played all our favorite songs and sang to me all the way home. He is no Barry White, but he was my prince charming.

When we got home, he blindfolded me and carried me inside the house. I heard the door close and felt his arms wrap around me.

"Today is all about you! I want to show you how happy I am that you are home," my husband whispered in my ear.

I smiled as he started to remove my blindfold. To my surprise, there were rose petals leading from the front door to the bathroom. My instructions were to get undressed and get in the tub. As I sat in the tub, my ever-so-detailed husband gave me a bath as soft music played in the background. After my bath, he wrapped me in a robe and carried me to our bed. We made the most passionate love with each other. Afterward, he held me, caressing my body with his gentle touches until we both fell asleep. I fell in love with my husband all over again that night.

Three weeks after my arrival home, it was time for my follow-up with my doctor to make sure I had not contracted anything during my deployment. After my physical and blood work, my provider asked me to stick around for a few minutes to go over the results with me. I sat in the lobby waiting on the doctor to finish up with her patients. I swear it felt like forever. If you are like me, I imagined every possible horrible disease that I may have contracted while in Iraq.

The nurse finally took me out of my misery and called me back to the doctor's office. The doctor told me to sit down because she wanted to go over some blood work information with me. As I braced myself for the worse possible news ever, I heard her say in the most angelic voice, "Congratulations, you are going to be a mother!"

I literally froze. You know how in the movies you are in the same room with someone, and they are talking to you, but you only see their lips moving, but you do not hear anything coming from their mouth. It's as if they are talking in slow motion. Well, that is what it was like for me after I heard those eight words. All I remember is getting a referral from my provider to see an OBGYN to start the journey to having a baby.

The drive home was surreal. On the one hand, I was so excited to be having a baby for my husband of ten years. On the other hand, I was so scared because nothing in our goals pertained to having a baby. We always promised each other that we would be financially and emotionally ready before having a baby. I was so scared to go home and tell him, because I did not know what his reaction was going to be.

I pulled into the garage and turned the engine off. Before I stepped out of the car, I prayed that the Lord would put the right words in my mouth to share this news with my husband. I walked up the stairs, opened the door, and called my husband's name. He walked into the living room and sat down next to me. I held his hands and looked in his eyes.

"I have something to share with you," I said as my voice crackled.

He stared into my eyes and said, "No matter what you say to me right now, baby, we will get through this together."

Looking at him with a blank stare, I quietly said the only words that came to mind, "Congratulations, you are going to be a father!" I gave him a moment to process the information. It was the longest silence ever between us. When he didn't say anything, I asked, "What are you thinking?"

He finally smiled at me and asked, "Are you OK with this?

"Yes, as long as you are OK."

We held each other on the couch. But as I lay in his arms and listened to his heartbeat, I felt something was wrong. As a woman, our intuitions are always right. For a moment, I thought I was overthinking things and should just give him time to process his emotions. We ended up falling asleep on the couch wrapped in the most awkward silence.

The next morning, we had breakfast at the table and finally started talking to each other. I had never seen my husband so lost for words. In the back of my mind, I knew he wanted to tell me something, but he just did not know how to put the words together to say what he wanted. We decided that I was going to keep the baby. Some of our plans and goals had to be put aside until our child was born. Our travel plans were on hold so we could start the process of purchasing a house.

I had a hair appointment scheduled, so I excused myself from the table and headed out the door. When I reached the hair salon, I put the car in park. As I was getting ready to step out the door, a tall, light-skin female approached me and stood right by the hood of the car.

"What are you doing driving this car?" she said sternly as she glared at me.

I had never seen this female before. The first thing I thought to myself was that she had mistaken me for someone else. "Excuse me! You have the wrong person. This is my car."

"I know this car and plate number anywhere. This is AC's car, and I have been riding in it for over three months now."

Well, at that point, I realized this female clearly knew my husband and apparently had been riding in this car for a while. In the harshest voice I could muster up I said, "This is *my* husband's car, and I am Mrs. AC. Apparently, you don't know about me. In a split second, her face got so pale as she looked at me in shock.

"I'm sorry. I did not realize AC was married. I have been dating him for the past three months, and I have never seen you," she said calmly.

"That's because I was deployed for a year and just got back," I explained. I invited her to sit with me at a nearby café so we could talk. She took me up on my offer, so we headed to the café. We each got a drink, and I began asking questions that I wanted answers to.

"How did you meet my husband?"

"We met at a local club on a Friday night and exchanged phone numbers. I asked him if he was single, and he told me he was. He continued to buy me drinks for the remainder of the night. We danced and had a good time. At the end of the night, he walked me to my car and asked if he could see me the next day. Of course, I said yes and then drove home."

As she continued to give me exact details about what had been going on between them, I felt like I was in the twilight zone. At some point during the conversation, I hoped someone would pinch me to wake me up. *This cannot be real!* I kept thinking to myself as I listened to this young lady tell me about *my* husband. I finally asked the question that had weighed on my heart for the longest time, although I was afraid to hear the answer.

"Have you been intimate with my husband?"

She answered in a low, meek voice, "Yes, we have."

Shocked by her response, I asked, "Where?"

"At his house," she said in the same meek tone.

At this point, I was so upset that I just wanted to curl up and cry. I explained to this female that we have been married for over five years and together for ten years. I was deployed to Iraq for a year. So apparently, he found himself getting into situations he should not have.

"I had no idea he was married. I will not be contacting him anymore," she said.

"Thank you for sitting with me and going over the details of your relationship with my husband. I know it wasn't easy." She stood and headed towards the door. I watched her walk to her car. With every step she took, I felt as if she was stepping on my heart.

I gathered myself together and canceled my hair appointment. On the drive home, I felt myself going through several emotions as if I was on a roller coaster ride. From getting angry, to crying, to being extremely livid, my emotions were all over the place. I had no idea what I was going to say or do once I arrived home and faced my husband.

I pulled into the driveway. All I could do was break down and cry. I have always been the strong person who never showed my true emotions. I keep a smile on my face and never let anyone know when they have hurt me or have made me angry. A long time ago, my grandmother taught me to "never let them see you sweat." For me to break down and cry and feel practically helpless was a new feeling for me, and I did not know how to handle these emotions.

I sat in the car for an hour and contemplated my next steps very carefully. I went over and over in my head the words I wanted to say when I got in the house. I finally mustered up enough strength to get out of the car and go inside. With every step that I took towards the front door, I felt my heart racing faster and faster. When I opened the door, I sat in the living room and waited for my husband to come out of the shower.

"Babe, how come your hair is not done? I thought you went to the shop," my husband said as he walked into the room.

With the limited strength I had left after crying for so long, I said, "Sit down so we can talk."

As my husband sat down, he looked at me and realized I was crying. He immediately dropped to his knees in front of me, held my hands, and in a somber voice, said, "Are you Ok? Is something wrong with the baby? Nadia, please speak to me."

I lifted my head, and with all the strength I could muster up, I glared at him and said, "What have you been doing while I was deployed in Iraq?" Before he could even open his mouth to answer, I said, "Before you ask me what I am talking about, or even think of lying to me, please don't."

He looked at me with a blank stare on his face as if he was trying to figure out what I was talking about.

Before he said a word, I asked, "Who is Melissa?"

His eyes opened wide, staring at me. The shocked look on his face was as if he saw a ghost when I asked that question. He suddenly released my hands, got up from his knees, and sat back on the couch with his head down.

This was the second time in our entire marriage that there was such a long silence between us. You could hear a pin drop in the room. I could tell that he was trying to figure out how I knew about Melissa. I finally broke our silence and said, "Please do not insult me by trying to think of a story to tell me just to avoid telling me the truth. You know that our marriage has always been built on trust and faith," I continued. "So, please, do not break what we have built by lying to me right now."

Taking a deep breath, my husband looked at me and said, "Babe, I am not sure what you know, but please give me a moment to explain myself to you. I am sure you probably think you know the entire story, but I can explain everything." He paused and took another deep breath, and said, "I am so sorry! I know I have messed up. I am willing to do anything to get you to forgive me."

Tears rolled down his face as he extended his hands for me to hold. "I did cheat on you while you were deployed. I was feeling lonely, and Melissa provided the companionship I was looking for while you were not here."

With every word he said, I felt my heart breaking into little pieces, as if it was a puzzle coming apart. He fell to his knees and put his head on my lap.

"Please forgive me! We can work this out. I want our family to be together," he said meekly.

Without saying a word, I removed his head from my lap and headed to the shower. As the hot water splashed over my body, tears streamed down my face. After my shower, I lay down, staring into the darkness, wishing the pain, and hurt would go away. This was the first time in our marriage that we had gone to bed in silence.

The next morning, I could barely open my eyes because they were swollen shut from crying all night.

"Baby, please talk to me," my husband said, gently pulling me towards him. "What can I do to make this better?"

"We need to go to counseling to figure out how we can work this out. I do not want to lose my family."

"I agree, Baby. I don't want to lose our family either." Within a week, he scheduled our first session. We went to counseling for three months to fix our marriage.

One Friday evening, I was home alone watching a movie, while my husband was at work. It was storming so badly and was pitch black outside. I was startled when the phone rang.

"Hello." There was silence on the other line. I said, "Hello, is anyone there?" I could hear the muffled sound of a person gasping for air between whimpers. I waited in silence, thinking, *Who is this?*

Finally, a female voice said, "This is Melissa. I want you to know I am pregnant by your husband."

As soon as I heard those words, the thunder rolled so hard and loud that it shook my home, and a bolt of lightning flashed in the sky. My heart felt like it shattered in pieces. I dropped the phone, and my knees started trembling. I felt so weak that I fell to the floor. Holding

27

my face in the palm of my hands, I cried uncontrollably as tears poured down my face.

After I composed myself, I picked the phone up to see if she was still on the phone, but she had hung up.

My husband came home a few minutes later and saw me on the floor crying. He ran over to me, picked me up, and sat me on the couch. Worried, he looked at me and said, "What's wrong? Is anything wrong with the baby?"

"Melissa is pregnant," I said softly, my voice weak from emotional exhaustion.

"I know. I did not know how to tell you," he said.

"You knew? I yelled. An intense burning rushed throughout my body. I couldn't hold back the anger anymore. "I don't want to hear anything else you have to say," I screamed.

I dashed into the kitchen and got some trash bags, went to the bedroom, and started throwing all his clothes in them.

"Nadia, please do not do this," he said frantically.

I turned around, looked him in his eyes, and yelled as loud as I could, "We are over! Do not ask me to forgive you for this, because I cannot! I will not accept you are having a baby with someone else. I want you to take all of your things and get out of my life forever!"

My husband had never seen me this angry. He knew not to say anything else to me. I continued packing all his clothes and threw them over the balcony in the rain. When I was done, I gave him the key to the car he apparently was driving someone else around in, and said, "Take this key, and drive as far as you can from me, and never look back."

He picked up the bags of clothes, put them in the car, and drove off. I stood in the rain on the balcony and watch my entire life drive off and leave me.

The next morning, I received a call from my commander asking if I was ready to renew my contract for another four years with the military. I responded, "No, sir. I will not re-enlist anymore I will be retiring."

I made the decision to move back home with my parents to get my feet back on the ground and figure out what I was going to do with my future. Within a week, the moving company came and packed up my home. When they left, I sat in the middle of the living room floor, feeling as empty as my home. My entire future I had planned with my husband was no longer a reality. I lost my husband, my home, and military benefits.

I did not have a happy pregnancy. There was no photoshoot, baby shower, or gender reveal. Instead, I was going through a divorce and crying every night.

Three months passed before my husband contacted me. He didn't express any concern for my wellbeing. He simply said, "We need to get a divorce, because Melissa's parents want us to be married before the baby arrives."

What About Me? I thought to myself. I signed the divorce papers right after giving birth to our son.

After two years of getting used to being a single parent, I found myself looking in the bathroom mirror and realized I deserved to be happy. I took a course in graphic design. When I graduated, I started my own business, My Sister Keeper. From that day on, I never allowed anyone to control my destiny or my happiness.

AN UNLIKELY LOVE

TRINA SAN

"You have prostate cancer," the doctor said to my fiancé as we sat there intently. I thought *no! What! I just asked Maurice to move out of my house. He just started a new job. What's going to happen?* We sat there in disbelief. The doctor continued to inform us what the next steps were because it needed to be treated immediately.

When we received the news, we had been dating for three-and-a-half years by the time he received this diagnosis from the VA doctor. This was not something either of us planned or anticipated, but it needed to be addressed immediately. Neither of us knew what was going to happen next for us, but we both knew what I had said only days earlier.

Three years earlier, Maurice and I had met on an online dating service. I was apprehensive in meeting him because he had two under-aged children, two adult children, and two former wives. My children are grown, and I have grandchildren. I agreed to meet in person after communicating for a couple of weeks, our introduction was quite unusual for me. As I drove to our meeting location, I prayed, "God, please let this one be 'the one.'" I was tired of dating. I drove up to the store where we agreed to meet.

As I drove to the parking lot across the street, I watched Maurice walking on the sidewalk towards my car, smiling from ear to ear on this beautiful spring day.

When I parked the car, he exclaimed, "Get out of the car! Turn around! You're a pretty thang!"

I thought, Really? Please tell me this isn't him. Oh, my goodness, it is! Look at his clothes. I believe he is stuck in the '90s. Oh well, he looks a little over-dressed for a train ride and a walk, but I'm here now—just go on the date. You don't have to see him again.

I laughed as I shook my head, "You're a mess! I'm Trina." He introduced himself as Maurice and replied, "a chocolate mess." He grabbed my arm and escorted me across the street to the blue line station to await the train to come and proceeded on our first date. Before the train arrived, I noticed he was quite the gentleman as he made sure I walked on the inside while he stayed on the outside near oncoming traffic and was attentive to my needs.

Maurice was and is still a very confident man. I was cautious yet happy to be going out with a college man. I always thought I was not good enough to date someone who graduated with a four-year degree—I had a two-year degree.

The conversation we had on the train was great! Maurice made me laugh—which can be hard for me on a first date. We were amazingly comfortable with one another, but I was still cautious. My track record with dating was to attach myself to one person; then, when the relationship doesn't work out, I would be stuck—sad, mad, and alone. I consciously decided not to let that happen this time. So, I had a couple of other male "friends" that I was talking to and seeing. This was a way for me to enjoy dating and to get to know someone before I jumped in headfirst.

31

Once we got off the train, we grabbed lunch at the Epicenter downtown and walked to the Romare Bearden Park. We continued to have a wonderful time together. At one point, Maurice got a little cocky and thought it was a good idea to grab my hand. My response was to quickly shake his hand off mine and exclaim, "Give me my hand back! I don't know you like that!"

"You're mine!" he said.

"No, I'm not!" It's funny now, but I meant it and I was not laughing. I heard a pastor's wife say, we can't control who we fall in love with, so be careful how you are with the person you're dating. Imagine that. I always thought I had control over who I fell in love with, and I most certainly was not going to fall in love with a man who had two under-aged children with potential baby momma drama!

During our date, we found out that we knew some of the same people and places. I had always wanted to be with someone who could relate to living in this city. It was just icing on the cake that he knew my old neighborhood. We also discovered that we raised our older children in the same neighborhood when both of us were married. The longer we talked, the more we found we had in common. This was one of the longest dates I ever had. We didn't want the date to end, so we made plans to go dancing that evening. Dancing is one of my favorite activities, yet I didn't often get a chance to go because I didn't like going to clubs.

As we headed back to our starting location, I stopped and turned to face Maurice. "I'm sorry, but I won't be available the following weekend because I have a friend visiting from out of town."

Apparently, Maurice had already decided I was the "one." Looking at me passionately, he said, "Tell your 'friend' not to come."

Unfortunately for him, I did not feel the same, although I did enjoy myself thoroughly. We parted ways, and I headed home to prepare to go out that evening.

On the way home, I called a friend and my daughter to let them know how the date went and that I was okay—that was my usual routine when I went out on a first and second date. I really wanted to take things slow and continue to date, because before anyone could turn their head, I'd be talking about love, which is why I had to keep my options open.

That evening I put on a form-fitting wrap dress that fit like a glove and would have turned anyone's head. I arrived on time and looked around for Maurice's car but didn't see it. After five minutes, I called, "Where are you?"

"I'm about five minutes away. Go ahead in the club, and I'll join you as soon as I get there."

"Oh, I don't think you want me to go in the club without you in this dress, because you might not see me again."

I don't know if his car had wings like the Batmobile, but he was there faster than a jet, parked his car, and ran over to greet me. Maurice took my hands in his, looked me up and down, and smiled like a Cheshire cat. Then, we walked inside the club, arm-in-arm.

Although Maurice had two left feet and no rhythm, we had a wonderful evening dancing the night away. Watching him was amusing, yet endearing. He was, again, very confident in who he was.

Every evening he got off work, he called, and we would talk for hours. He didn't know it at the time, but every evening I was sound asleep and woke up just to talk to him. We shared information about ourselves, where we grew up, talked about our children, work, told

jokes, and just enjoyed getting to know one another. My biggest issue with this man was his two minor children. I was not interested
in raising more children since mine were adults with their own kids.
*Would I really be willing to start over raising children? Why would I
do that? You must be crazy—move on,* I thought, but I didn't.

Once Friday came, I was supposed to be preoccupied with an out-
of-town friend, but all I could think about was Maurice. My friends
reminded me to enjoy spending time with my guest since he was
coming all the way from Colorado. However, in the evening, I would
call Maurice. I kept telling myself, *Trina, you just met the man a week
ago. Stop thinking about him.*

The next few weeks were even more exciting than the first week.
We took walks, went to the movies, had lunch and/or dinner, attended concerts in Freedom Park, and went to bible study every
Wednesday. I couldn't believe he even asked me to go to church. I
dated several men who said they went to church and loved the Lord,
yet not one had asked me to go.

Eventually, I was invited to his home to meet his dog, Lucy. Lucy
was a Whippet mix who loved attention, and she was protective of
her master. One evening I was going to visit, and Lucy must have
known I was coming because she protested by pooping in her kennel. He didn't want me to come right away as he needed time to clean
her kennel. But within a few days, Lucy and I were best friends.

One afternoon, while having lunch, Maurice told me that he loved
me and wanted to make our relationship permanent. That was code
for "he didn't want me to date anyone else but him." He then proceeded to put a string on my finger and stated this was my 'promise
string' until he could get me a real ring. Yes, I said string. That was
the sweetest thing I had ever heard, and I wore that string every day
until I lost it. Words cannot express how sad it was for me when I

had lost the string. He did, however, replace that string with a ring many times over.

Our backgrounds could not have been more different. He grew up in a single-parent household along with a younger brother and was surrounded by other family members. His dad lived in another state, along with his older brother. He was a student of the Bible and started going to church when he was eight years old, without anyone telling him to go. He got in his share of trouble, like most boys do, but he never went to prison, was addicted to any substance, nor did he have any children as a teenager. He spent a lot of his time sitting in the house reading books while the other kids were running around getting into mischief. Maurice knew he wanted to get out of the projects, so he set his sights on college.

While Maurice came from humble beginnings, he had a strong will to do more with his life than some people he grew up around. He played sports through the Bethlehem Center—which also kept him out of trouble. Once he graduated high school, he attended and graduated from North Carolina Central University. After graduating, he found himself back in his old neighborhood, unable to find work, so he enlisted in the Marine Corps. Maurice secured a job, got married, and had children.

However, I grew up in a middle-class neighborhood with both parents. My mom was always at home unless she went shopping. There was always food on the table, and I never had to be concerned about the safety in my neighborhood. There weren't any children my age on my block, which meant I had to walk to either one of my two friends' homes or meet at the park to have someone to play with. When I was reading, it was from the Childcraft or the Black History books my dad purchased from a salesman. Some weekends my nephews or nieces would visit, and we played together, but most of the week was spent in the house watching TV with mom, roller skating, doing crafts, or playing with my dolls.

After we had been dating six months, Maurice moved in with me. I wish I could say after he moved in things were all sunshine and roses, but it wasn't. It started out okay since he worked a different shift. I was an early riser, and he went to bed late. I am a routine person, and I didn't like my bed not being made up in the morning, nor was I used to the television being on in the middle of the night or food being cooked while I slept. Oh yeah, it was okay in the very beginning because it was new, but when the newness wore off, it was insane.

I kept trying to figure out why I let a man come live with me when I knew it wasn't God's will for my life. I thought, *God does not approve of us living together.* I had so many things I wanted to do to help young women keep themselves unto God until they got married, and here I was, living in sin. Those thoughts kept me from accepting my decision and caused a lot of strife between us.

Maurice would tell me that I had it all wrong. God forgives me for my sin. I thought he was reading a different Bible than I was. I spent time with God every morning, and in my heart, I knew I was doing the wrong thing, but I loved this man and wanted to help him.

Over the next few years, we would argue, threaten to end the relationship, and then be back in one another's arms. This was very difficult for both of us, and it was tiring, but neither one of us wanted to end the relationship, so we went to counseling. If you want to see what's wrong with you, go to counseling. Those sessions revealed that we needed to end our relationship since we did not do the work our therapist had suggested. Counseling is effective if you do what is recommended. Although we wanted to improve our relationship, by the end of our third session, our counselor fired us.

I was fed up and didn't want to sit through that again, and neither did he. We continued to live together for the next two years. One day, while walking, Maurice fell when the neighbor's dogs were attempting to attack him and Lucy. After he fell, he began experiencing pain in his hand and ankle which required him to have surgery twice. These operations put even more strain on our relationship because Maurice was unable to work as he had previously. As a result, our financial situation changed dramatically. Maurice was stressed because he couldn't help much, and I was stressed because I had to pull money from resources that I didn't want to touch. I knew if I started my home-based business again, I could fill the gap financially—although I didn't want to do it again.

I prayed for God's guidance, and I knew I just needed to trust God to work it out. Consequently, it was my belief that God wouldn't provide since I was living in sin. But eventually, my prayers were answered. Maurice was healed enough to return to work, however, his job fired him because they did not receive the return-to-work letter. He discovered a letter was sent to his ex-wife's address, but he was never notified about the letter. Here he was in his late 50's looking for employment. Maurice can do anything and succeed if he wants to, and this was no different. He was excited when he finally found a job. He would have been a top-tier employee had he not received the sobering news that he had cancer.

The diagnosis of cancer changed our relationship. Maurice knew that he was causing me stress and pain, so he moved out before he began chemotherapy treatments. I didn't want him to go, but I didn't know how I was going to continue working, even if he had stayed. This was a very painful process for both of us. His ego wouldn't allow him to go back on his decision to leave. I was sad, but he didn't believe me. After weeks of going back and forth to gather his belongings, Maurice was gone from my life for the next eight months. Occasionally, he would send me a text to say hello or to let me know how he was doing. What I later found out was that he was on so much medication, he would sleep for days.

We reconnected the winter after Maurice had completed his chemotherapy. I was a little apprehensive because he was still the same person. I am time conscious, and he's not. I'm organized, and he's not—well, not like I am. I don't like clutter, and well, let's just say it doesn't bother him. We are so different, but somehow it works most of the time. The time together was nice—although I kept my guard up because I didn't want to be hurt again. Maurice later admitted neither did he. He said it then, and he still says it—he was sent by God for me. I used to think he was crazy, but I can see now how Maurice's presence and love have propelled me to grow out of my shell. It has also allowed me to see how big God really is. With that, we were again engaged.

During the next two years, he lived in my home, again, which did not go well. A few months later, Maurice moved into his own place. My plan was to move on with my life. I wanted to get this bad experience out of my mind and just live by myself again. However, I proceeded to assist Maurice in getting his home set up, as insane as this sounds. Before finishing, we had another disagreement which made me want to close the door permanently. I was tired of the ups and downs we were going through. I left his home angry and frustrated.

What I later came to understand is that when someone is in pain, perhaps men more than women, they take their frustration out on those who are closest to them. I should know that because when I'm hurt emotionally, I respond in the same manner.

I began to have more compassion for Maurice because he started to open up more to me about his feelings and the pain he was experiencing. We really wanted our relationship to grow into something beautiful, but we knew we needed guidance.

One Sunday, our church announced they were having a Marriage Dynamics class. Both of us had previously been married, and we really wanted our marriage to work. I admit there were many who thought we should not be married because of the inconsistency in our relationship. I believed them all, but I was going to give this class a shot. If it didn't work, then we could part ways for good.

Unfortunately, he was sick most of the time when we had to complete homework, but he never wanted to miss a class, no matter how bad he was feeling physically. There were some nights we would have an argument on the way to the class, but he would be fine after the class. However, I was still stuck on being angry and didn't want him to even look at me.

During one of the weeks in class, we learned about our "love language." As a result, we discovered we would need to speak one another's language if we wanted our love to grow. We learned Maurice's love language is quality time—watching sports, and sex. My love language is acts of service and quality time. Maurice and I would shop together, which was special to me. I would watch a sports game or two with him, and we grew closer. *Perhaps this love will really grow into something beautiful.*

In 2020, the year of the pandemic, while writing my first book, we were finally married. Although it was a small ceremony, it was perfect. God had his hand on our union. My son and daughter gave me away. Our friend and pastor married us at the Levine Cancer Center on November 14th in the presence of close friends and family.

There were others who participated in our wedding ceremony via Zoom. It could not have been a better day.

If we had given up on "us," we would not have the life we have today. My husband often tells me that I'm the reason he's still living. Maurice tells me every day how much he loves me and showers me with gifts. He also, watches a mushy drama with me, occasionally. I know that he's the reason I wrote and completed my book. Even from his bedside, Maurice has opened my eyes to real estate investing.

In 2015, I couldn't imagine raising minors, but today I'm glad that I get a chance to love on them and assist them in one day growing into young adults. They have all been a blessing to my life.

As I look in the mirror and reflect over my life, I realize the difficulties we experienced make this time we have together worth it!

AGELESS CONVERSATIONS

TAMIKA MCTIER

I remember being a freshman in college, sitting in class, and not feeling so well. The queasiness in the pit of my stomach was the same feeling I had been experiencing for a couple of days. I noticed that it was more prevalent during the morning hours. Not focused on anything that was going on in class that morning, a flash of fear suddenly came over me. I thought, *Could I be pregnant?* The possibility weighed heavily on me as I replayed the thought over and over in my head.

Once I finished classes for the day, I immediately made my way to the doctor. I was relieved that I could walk in without an appointment. I went straight to the lab and requested a blood test. A regular pregnancy test wouldn't do; I needed accuracy. So, after having my blood drawn, the cause of my morning nausea was confirmed. I was indeed pregnant.

A small amount of fear came over me as I wondered what would happen once I told my mom. What was my boyfriend going to say? How would people view me? Could I even care for a child? As the daughter and sister of teen mothers, I knew the odds were stacked against me. Teen pregnancy was so common in the '90s; I saw it all around me. I had convinced myself that I would never become a teenage pregnancy statistic, yet here I was pregnant at eighteen.

41

I made up my mind to have my baby. Nothing was going to stop me from thriving at this thing called life and becoming a mom. With the support of my mother and boyfriend, I went in full throttle. This life-altering event completely changed my outlook, and my mindset shifted. I realized that even if I was going to become a teen mom, I was still the narrator of my story and could change the narrative. I was not destined to be a statistic. I was determined to go to work and school. Teen motherhood would also not stop me from accomplishing my goal of becoming a college graduate.

My pregnancy was going well until week twenty-eight when suddenly my blood pressure became really high, and my doctor advised me to work less. By week thirty, my blood pressure had continued to rise, and I was placed on bed rest. A week later, my condition got worse, and I was admitted to the hospital. Diagnosed with toxemia, I was faced with giving birth weeks before my due date. I was filled with all kinds of emotions. Was I ready? Was my boyfriend? We didn't even know the sex of our child.

July 12th arrived, and it was my nineteenth birthday. I was experiencing some contractions, but nothing strong or consistent enough to put me in labor. By the following evening, things quickly spiraled out of control. My blood pressure became dangerously high, making an emergency C-section necessary.

And on July 14th, my baby girl, Jasmine, was born. This little girl shifted my whole world and became my focus. There wasn't room for much else, so it wasn't much of a surprise when my relationship with my boyfriend ended shortly after my daughter's birth. Like my mom, I was also a single mother.

Though my parents' relationship was unsuccessful, my dad was always someone I could turn to for laughter. He never missed an opportunity to tell me he loved me, which always made me smile. As his only child, he bragged about me often to family and friends. I was confident that my boyfriend would have a great relationship with our daughter no matter what. So, though our relationship ended, just like my father, he has always remained active in our daughter's life.

Teen motherhood had its challenges. My mother knew those challenges all too well. Her strength and support showed me that even though the journey would be difficult, it wasn't impossible. This life-defining event was the first of many to teach me that our challenges refine us if we let them. I learned that the way we approach our problems is the way we move through them. With each challenge I've faced, I've had something to prove to myself. I realized that to thrive in life, I needed to have a sound foundation in my faith, fitness, finances, and family. These pillars have become the core foundation of who I am today.

FAITH

"Train a child in the way he should go, and when he is old, he will not depart from it." Proverbs 22:6

One of my earliest childhood memories includes me attending church with my mother. I recall enjoying the choir music and giving speeches at Easter. We went regularly but weren't particularly religious. Then suddenly, it just stopped. I don't know why, but I don't remember us ever going to church during my high school years. Once I became a mom, I felt a tug. Something was missing. I wanted to go back to church, but I did not know where to start and was afraid to ask anyone.

Then one day at work, I overheard my co-worker describe how she went to church and enjoyed the service. Still feeling the tug to get back to church and learn more about God, I plied her with several questions, including if she planned to go on the upcoming Sunday.

She assured me she would be there and invited me to come along. I anxiously accepted and joined her.

I can't remember what the message was that Sunday, but I will always remember how I felt. Living life as a single mom, sometimes I felt lonely and defeated. But, when I entered the church, I instantly experienced a sense of joy come over me. From the greetings to the praise team and the pastor's sermon, I was at home. I did not know what I needed until I received it. I am forever grateful my mother introduced me to God and the church at an early age. After attending that one service, I knew this was what I needed and wanted more. So, I committed to attending weekly.

"Therefore, if anyone is in Christ, he is a new creation." 2 Corinthians 5:17

Soul-care is self-care and connecting back to my faith was one of the best ways I could feed my soul. I remember being in church one Sunday, and during the time when members are invited to dedicate themselves to Christ, I heard a voice say, *"Now it's your time."* I knew it was the Holy Spirit. Somewhat fearful, I asked my co-worker who was sitting beside me if she would walk with me. She enthusiastically accepted. At that moment, I felt a sense of relief as I dedicated my life back to Christ.

A few weeks into my new relationship, I knew that going to church once a week would not be enough for me. So, I was intentional about getting involved in ministry, spending time reading my Bible, and making impactful friendships that aligned with my spiritual goals. One such friend and I became prayer partners, spending time with God every morning at 5:30 am. I made the commitment to know my Creator for myself. Consequently, my faith soared. I saw firsthand that He was my shepherd and my provider. He became more than just my backup plan, but my *first* plan. I learned to see

Him as more than a God in my valleys but on my mountain tops, too. Through prayer and reading the Bible, I learned there was nothing I couldn't go to God about. Through my relationship with God, I could forgive myself and release all the shame I carried from becoming a teen mom and wondering what others thought of me. I WAS FREE!

FINANCES

When I graduated high school, my mother gifted me $1,000 in cash. While my mom had always shown me what it looked like to work hard, I was so excited and never expected her to give me that type of gift. What might not be a lot of money to some was a lot of money to me, especially knowing the sacrifices my mother made for me as a single parent.

At seventeen years old, I was so ecstatic about receiving this small fortune; I told my mom that I didn't want to spend it. So, she encouraged me to open a savings account. I did and immediately started stashing away the money I made from my job.

Financial security is financial freedom and independence. I strived for both, not based on what I was told but on what I saw. As a child, I witnessed my father abuse my mother. At the time, I couldn't understand why she stayed, but later I learned of the incredible strength she had to leave him and build an independent life. She worked hard to provide for me, and I soon realized for myself that what I could build on my own, no man could take away.

Once I learned about my pregnancy, I knew I wanted to be financially independent. I felt like I had already become a statistic by getting pregnant at eighteen and immediately adopted a mindset to do everything possible to financially provide for my child. Sure, it would have been easy for me to get public assistance, but I did not want that. Plus, I felt this was what society would expect since I saw so many people around me get on assistance and never get off it. Securing myself financially by working and saving money seemed to be the best option.

"A wise man saves for the future." Proverbs 21:20

Although my introduction to saving money came from my mother's gift, my WHY and mindset shift for saving money became clear with motherhood. I knew that I never wanted to be in a position where I wondered where money was coming from. So, I decided I would continue my education and pick up more hours at work to increase my savings. At the time, I had a minimum wage job. Thankfully, I didn't have any expenses since I was still living at home. So, I started saving even more of my paychecks.

Once I had my daughter, I knew I needed to make more money. I started working at a bank as a teller, and I really enjoyed it. However, one Friday morning, after I'd been working there for six months, three armed men entered the bank with masks covering their faces. I found myself in the middle of a full-blown "Set-It-Off" type of robbery. Afterward, I spent the entire weekend shaken and too terrified to do anything, especially since the guys had not been caught.

When I returned to work, I immediately told my manager that I intended to resign. The robbery shook me, and I wanted out. My manager said I was a valued employee and told me to give her a couple of days. Later, she came back and presented me with a promotion that would give me a pay increase and a more suitable set schedule. I immediately accepted the role. Though the robbery was traumatic, this was just another life challenge that I was determined not to let define me. From this horrifying event came a great opportunity, and I fully intended to move forward and take advantage of it.

That promotion was the first of many I would earn during my years in banking. Working at the bank, I learned the importance of credit. I used that knowledge to increase my financial situation for my daughter and me. Eventually, I was able to purchase a brand-new car, giving me something reliable to get around.

Getting a new car was a great way for me to establish my credit. Two years after purchasing my car, my credit was finally good enough to strike out on my own. Up until this point, I had always lived at home with my mom and commuted to school. But now, I decided, I was ready to spread my wings. So, my daughter and I moved into our first two-bedroom apartment.

Though I loved having a place of my own, I grew restless after two years of living in that apartment. My daughter and I were slowly outgrowing the space, and my lease was coming up for renewal. At twenty-four, I was still consistent with saving and had built up a substantial amount of money, so I considered buying a house. I wanted to give my daughter the chance to grow up in a home in a neighborhood where she could play with her friends. And I refused to let being a young single mother be a barrier to this dream. I knew I did not have to be married or wait on a man to become a homeowner, so I reached out to a loan officer to get pre-qualified. After looking at several homes, I finally found one I loved, and the location was perfect. The sellers accepted my offer, and I closed on my first home a few weeks after my twenty-fifth birthday.

Over twenty years later, I am still diligent about saving money, and now I have included investments.

FITNESS

The first promotion from being a bank teller was in an operations department. There was a lady in the department who would always call me her daughter. I guess she felt a certain affinity for me since her daughter and I were the same age. I admired her, as she was a very poised woman. I noticed she always went to the gym during her lunch hour, which was convenient since a gym was located right in the building for employees. One day, I asked her a few questions about what she did at the gym, and she invited me to join her. I agreed. Agreeing to join her at the gym every day during lunch was the beginning of me making fitness a lifestyle.

I was first introduced to fitness as a young child when my mom would take me along with her and her friends to aerobics class. Still, it hadn't become a routine part of my life. However, having that scare with high blood pressure during my pregnancy, I knew I never wanted to face that again. I wanted to take control of my health.

Fitness is one way in which I express love and kindness to my body. I not only enjoy it, but it also serves as a way for me to release stress and show up for myself. Although working out gives me an outward appearance that I like, it's the feeling that I get from serotonin and endorphin releases that keeps me committed and consistent.

It has been over twenty years, and I am still committed to being healthy mentally and physically. My journey has included one-on-one training, group fitness, kickboxing, and completing countless 5ks, 10k's, six half-marathons, a relay full-marathon with four other women, and a 200-mile race with eleven other women. I love anything that creates a challenge and community.

"Exercise should be a celebration for what your body can do, not punishment for what you ate." —Unknown

There was a time when I lived by the number on the scale, and I did anything to achieve what I felt was the right number. But mentally, I found this method very stressful. I never sensed that diet, culture, and food deprivation would be a lifestyle I could maintain.

As I look back, I realize that being a slave to my weight created fear. I wanted freedom. When I realized how negatively the scale made me feel, I made a mindset shift once again. I turned my focus to maintaining consistency with my workouts, eating for fuel, and paying attention to the way my clothes fit. When I shifted my mindset from what I weighed to how I felt daily, I felt much better overall.

Do I still weigh myself? Yes! But it might be once every couple of months. Being healthy does not equate to a look. Fitness for me is more than the outward appearance and the number on the scale. It's proper sleep, solitude, connection, faith, and work that helps me to relieve stress and maintain a healthy mental state.

FAMILY

When I separated from my daughter's father, I spent years just casually dating, but it never produced anything meaningful. Getting into a committed relationship was not something I spent time focused on. I was more interested in dating with a purpose versus getting heavily involved with someone just to say I was in a relationship. However, that all changed one Friday evening, in April 2004, when I met my husband over the phone during a quick conversation.

After being a homeowner for a little less than a year, I had received an escrow check in the mail. I called inquiring about the legitimacy of the check and if it was safe for me to cash. Thomas was the person who assisted me and informed me that after conducting some research on his end, I could cash the check. We exchanged laughter as I made a couple of jokes about how I would respond if he were not telling me the truth. Then the conversation ended.

The bank that held my mortgage was the same bank I worked for, so Thomas was essentially my co-worker. The following Monday morning, I received an email from him asking how my weekend was.

I thought it was odd that he reached out to me, but I didn't hesitate to respond. We exchanged phone numbers and began daily email and phone conversations outside of work. This went on for six weeks, and while we worked for the same employer in the same building, we had never seen one another.

I'm a very inquisitive person, so I had a list of questions every day to ask him. Our conversations were so rich, and I could feel the connection growing each time we talked. We had built an indescribable friendship in such a short amount of time. I remember asking him if he had kids or if he'd ever dated someone with kids. He replied "no" to both questions; then I informed him I had a child. I was pleased that he didn't seem to have a problem with that and wanted to get to know me more.

I was just waiting for him to ask, *"When can I meet you face-to-face?"* So, when he finally did, I immediately responded, "NOW! Come to my desk now and meet me." He agreed, and with excitement and nervousness, I waited with anticipation to see this guy I had silently fallen in love with yet had never seen before. Thinking back to some of the morning prayers I had with God, I wondered if Thomas could be an answered prayer or if it was possible to love someone I had never seen. What if there was no physical attraction?

I soon learned that I had nothing to worry about. When we met, we found each other attractive, and both wanted to continue what we had started. We became a couple. At the time, I had only shared my experience of meeting Thomas with one good friend. She would always tell me how much I smiled when I spoke of him.

"For this reason, a man shall leave his father and his mother and be joined to his wife, and they shall become one flesh." Genesis 2:24

By October 2004, we knew we wanted to spend the rest of our lives together. While some thought we were moving fast, we never let that stop us. On February 12th, 2005, Thomas planned a surprise engagement party with our friends and family. He got down on one knee, read a poem, and asked me to marry him. Without hesitation, I said, "YES!" We got married on September 3rd, 2005. After eight years, I was no longer a single parent.

I got pregnant during our honeymoon, and in May 2006, I gave birth to our son, Jalen. My marriage has truly been more than I could ask or imagine it would be.

A dream deferred doesn't have to die.

After years of stopping and starting school to concentrate on working and raising my daughter, I finally completed college and earned my Bachelor of Business Administration. I believe women are more than the totality of their age and their experiences. After becoming a mom at age nineteen, I could have used that experience as an excuse to stop me from accomplishing anything I wanted to achieve in life. Instead, I used every obstacle presented before me as an opportunity to prove that I could do it. Every decision I made to get to the next level was necessary for me to transform my mind, assess my foundation, learn new techniques, and kick-start the confidence that I could do anything I worked for. I knew that God would give me the desires of my heart according to his plans for my life. God has used my experiences and marriage as a way for me to connect with women and be the trusted source for those who seek advice, words of encouragement, prayer, and empowerment.

Today, I am a thriving wife of sixteen years, mom of two, certified marriage facilitator, speaker, life coach, and host of the Ageless Conversations podcast. And where is the baby who started my whole journey? She is a strong, educated, and independent woman who, through my life's lessons, has broken cycles and lives without barriers.

AFFIRMATIONS

I am resilient

I am a seed that bears fruit

I am love and light

I am the physical essence of God

I will accomplish all that I am purposed to do

Write your personal affirmation/s here:

SECTION 2

FRACTURED FOUNDATION

Children are dependent on the foundation of the family unit to nurture them to lead healthy lives. But what happens when the foundation is fractured or broken, and the cracks follow them into adulthood? At what point do they recognize they own the power to fill those cracks with the golden glue of God's light?

But Jesus said, "Suffer little children, and forbid them not, to come to me: for of such is the kingdom of heaven." Matt 19:14 King James Version

NOT AN OPTION! LEAVE NOW OR DIE

ALLISON G DANIELS

"The Lord said to Abram: Leave your country, your family, and your relatives and go to the land that I will show you" Genesis 12:1 CEV (Contemporary English Version).

Have you ever wondered how you got from a point "A" position to a point "Z" position without life taking you out, or you throwing in the towel, so to speak? Well, let me share with you that I grew up in a household where there were nineteen family members living under one roof. Yes, you read correctly, nineteen. We were a dysfunctional family, and the word dysfunctional is an understated word. In fact, it minimizes the accuracy of fully describing our living environment. Sadly, there was so much going on under our roof—the drinking, smoking, the fighting, and so much more. This went on, continuously, day in and day out. It was overwhelming to witness.

The problems we encountered were a family history of sibling jealousy and rivalry, family secrets of cheating, a history of nervous breakdowns, suicidal attempts, and depression, just to name a few. In addition, I had a child out of wedlock at the age of twenty-five. My daughter's father said no one would ever want me. In fact, he didn't even show up for the birth of our beautiful daughter.

Consequently, all of this forced me to make a decision about my life, because continuing in this manner was not an option. I had to either leave or die! I realized I had to make a change quickly, however not knowing when or the right time to do so was disheartening. But I knew I did not want my daughter growing up in a toxic "family" derived out of hatred, bitterness, and brokenness. At the time, I could not see the light at the end of the tunnel. Soon after my daughter was born, I contemplated my next steps. I knew, as a single mom, I had to put all my dreams, specifically college, on hold because I wanted to make a difference for my daughter.

As a young mother, I was greatly troubled over the pain, the hurt, and the afflictions of which so many of my family members suffered through the years. However, I was warned long ago by my family that what goes on in our home stays in our home. Yet this was the very place that was trying to kill me. This was the place where I was held in bondage by fear of moving on, the fear of breaking this dysfunctional cycle; the fear of breaking the generational curse; and the fear of a financial-lack mentality in my bloodline. Yet, I stayed and remained silent for years, and I never sought out what God had for my daughter and me.

As strong as I was, I was still vulnerable to what my family was saying to me as well as some of the negative comments that were spoken over me before I gave birth to my daughter. I realized that one of the hardest things for me to do was to speak with someone about what I was going through or even what I was feeling concerning the entrapment and the painful experiences that I had witnessed in my own household, my own life. Although I spent many nights trying to block out the yelling, the name-calling, and the cursing, I was too ashamed to tell anyone. So, I carried the guilt of my family's sad and disruptive encounters with me for a long time, wondering if there was something more that I could have done.

There are so many people who are hurting from what has been ingrained in them for many years, i.e., what their family and friends have spoken over them, what they have done, and what they have taught them as they were growing up. So many were never able to break away from the everyday dysfunctional family norm. However, I realize now that my brokenness before God was of value, and that God could use me if I stepped out in faith and just trust Him. But again, my brokenness tried to ruin me—to leave me powerless. Essentially, my brokenness became my bravery, my boldness, and my shield of protection, which helped me mend the disturbed and fractured pieces of my life.

I had so many mixed emotions on my life's journey because I had been down this road before. You see, it was during the most difficult times in my life that I finally heard God speak to me, and God told me to uproot my life with my daughter and leave everything that was familiar.

One day I felt the pains of life pouring over my spirit. I had suffered at the hands of those individuals whom I truly cared about and loved. I felt as if I didn't want to live anymore because so much was coming at me all at once. It was in my moments of doubt that I felt God's hand on my situation. I remember constantly meditating on God's Word, "I have been crucified with Christ and I no longer live, but Christ lives in me. The life I now live in the body, I live by faith in the Son of God, who loved me and gave himself for me" (Galatians 2:20). I had to stand on God's promises and His Word and never let it go.

I remember waking up one morning and not wanting to leave my house because the devil had convinced me that the whole world hated me; that the whole world was against me because I was finally walking away from my family. Before leaving, I had to have a serious heart-to-heart talk with my mother.

57

"I'm leaving and I'm never coming back! But mom, I thank you for everything you and dad have done for me and my daughter. But before I ever come back here, I will go into a shelter.

"Why?" she asked.

"Because there are some unhandled issues within this family that need to be addressed that are being swept under the rug, and no one wants to talk about them. So, I'm removing my daughter and myself from this environment. As a family, we tend to dismiss our feelings of anger, frustration, and bitterness. We fear seeking help. But mom, this will not be my story, because I'm changing the narrative and re-writing my own storyline."

My family situation was destroying me internally. I felt as if God wasn't listening to me anymore. I was in a valley of dry bones, and I felt like God was far from me. My faith was under attack. Everything that I had learned in my life about God and His Word was under attack. In addition to my already challenging life, people who called themselves my friends turned on me. Also, my family members rebelled against me, hurting me physically and mentally. So, eventually, I reached a point of brokenness, because I felt as if I could not go on.

I began to understand God was changing things right before my eyes. Yet, this old flesh wanted me to back down in fear. I realized that God's Word was placed inside of me to use and call on His name. "In my distress, I called to the Lord; I cried to my God for help. From his temple he heard my voice; my cry came before him, into his ears" (Psalms 18:6 NIV). I needed healing for my soul. I knew God was able to repair and restore to me the things in my life that I had lost along the way.

As I was being restored in my spirit, God was bringing me to a new level of peace and joy in my life. I had a made-up mind that I was one of the ones who was going to make it out of this hell that I called my home. I didn't want my daughter to grow up hearing negative things, especially from her dad. So, yes, I walked away, and I never looked back because the mentality that my family was living under and being consumed by was not what God wanted for me. The image and likeness I had of being God's daughter was different.

I recall waking up early one morning. I glanced out the door and saw my spirit man walk away. What I mean by that is I saw my spirit release itself from my body, look back at me, and walk out the door. Now, I tell you, this wasn't the first time this had happened to me. Initially, I didn't know what it meant until I felt peace and calmness come over me. I knew I wasn't in that negative space anymore. I knew that my God had called me to move on—to move forward with peace in Him.

Suddenly, I started remembering what my mother used to say to me when I was a young child growing up. She would tell me, *"Baby, you were born with a veil over your face."* And I asked her, *"What does that mean?"* My mother replied, *"You can see things before they happen."* Hearing that as a child truly frightened me. But, this time, I cried out to God, and I sought Him for the answers I needed because I was lost for words. My perspective about the problem was replaced with stress, anxiety, and fear, but I wasn't going to change my position about my love and trust in God. Despite everything I was going through in my life, I still trusted God. I still believed God was able to change my situation. Somehow, I knew there was nothing impossible for God to change for me, His daughter, Allison. He would break the code of silence, and He would break the code of staying in a house where I was not loved, wanted, or needed.

The Word of God says, "Be strong and of a good courage; be not afraid, neither be thou dismayed: for the Lord thy God is with thee whithersoever thou goest," (Joshua 1:9 KJV). I prayed for God to bring comfort, peace, and quietness to my weary soul. I had to stop focusing on my situation and had to remember that goodness and mercy follows me all the days of my life. So, I started looking forward to great things that would come to pass in my life, but in God's timing.

So, I resigned from the cares of this world, and I fully gave my life over to God, because I realized then that He was starting to cleanse and purge some things out of my life. God needed to get rid of the things that were not of Him, and He needed to mend my broken spirit. A mighty shift was taking place in my life. God was shifting things around in my mind for the better. I wasn't thinking the same way anymore. God was moving things around in my heart; He was giving me a heart of flesh and removing the stony heart. God was preparing me for the ministry that He placed on my heart, which was to minister to the hurting so that they could be healed, delivered, and set free. God was getting me ready to be strengthened and empowered to handle the cares of this world towards His people.

Finally, three years later, in June of 1997, I left my family's home. God blessed me tremendously and allowed me to meet my husband, which truly has been one of the many blessed and best things that have ever happened to me. One day I started sharing with him everything that I held inside–everything that was going on.

He responded, "Allison, hold your head up high! Your family let you down. No matter what you were trying to do, they were always against you trying to help others in your family to do the right thing. Your family let *you* down. Even when you told me that your daughter's father told you that nobody would want a woman who already had a child, you, my love, defied all the odds.

Not only have you defied all the odds, but you enrolled in that bachelor's degree program. Now, at age fifty-three, you have earned your BS degree. In 2014, you were licensed as Reverend Allison G. Daniels. In addition to those accomplishments, you have written over thirty-one books. You are the visionary author of three books and co-authored twelve books. And in 2013, God birthed your ministry, Allison Daniels' Ministries. In 2019, God also birthed your publishing company, AGD Publishing. As if that wasn't enough, God sustained you to work in the Federal government for so many challenging years—for thirty-seven plus years.

See Al, you, my dear, are that woman they said would not amount to anything. You are that woman who God has manifested His change in your life. You were so busy helping others, nourishing others, trying to keep the family together that you didn't know your own strength or the myriad of accomplishments. But you were changing lives along the way and touching people who you didn't know you had touched because you did it unselfishly."

My husband had gently reminded me of my accomplishments in Christ, notably, by the favor and hand of Almighty God.

As I reflect on the past, I realize now that I had to take a leap of faith and believe I could make it and not ever wonder what I would have left behind. Eventually, it all came full circle for me in that God had ordered my steps and anointed the assignments that would take place in my life.

I realized it was God speaking to me. He was getting ready to restore order back into my life. I believed that it was time for me to get closer to God. As a child of God, a daughter of God, I had to take my hands off my life and allow God to defend me. I knew my heart needed to be in tune with God for me to hear His voice, and His voice only. I needed to be in a place where He could use me "more" effectively in a way that would show His divine workmanship. I asked

God to humble me so I could see His hand working in various areas in my life. I completely surrendered to Him.

The narrative over my life had finally been changed. I kept moving and walking in my own authority, which was indeed ordered by the Lord. I was speaking in pulpits, a myriad of conventions, writing books, and helping many women get healed, delivered, and set free, unmistakably by the Word and hand of God. God used me as a willing vessel to bring Him glory and honor. God blessed me to be a blessing to my parents as their caregivers, so they wouldn't have to live in an assisted living facility. He has also allowed me to be a blessing to my immediate and extended families. Truly, God has blessed our entire household. For every mountain God brought me over, I could finally see the light, God's light shining bright on me. I could finally see the light at the end of the tunnel.

Now, I invite you to see me, the woman many said would never amount to anything. Look at me now! My husband also reminded me to look at all the dreams that God sent my way. He said, "Look at the vast number of people God has blessed you to pour into here on the earth and see how it has manifested. Lives have been changed, and they are still changing because you are helping people tell their stories; you are being a blessing to others."

I had not realized just how much I had overcome because I was in the center of it all. But now I see that I overcame lack, low self-esteem, shame, guilt, depression, and anxiety, just to name a few. But God! From time to time, we all face situations that seem impossible, but I now realize that God was working a multitude of things out on my behalf.

In spite of all I had gone through, God was birthing many ministries within me and through me. I continue to do Facebook "Live" at

5:00 am every Monday morning. I am also blessed to host two podcasts: The Authors' Lab where I interview business owners and Authors Chat with Allison, interviewing new and upcoming authors.

I believed that God had my best interests at heart. I promised God I would set my mind on things above and not on things of this earth (See Colossians 3:2). I made up my mind that I was going to trust in the Lord with all my heart and not lean unto my own understanding (See Proverbs 3:5). I just needed to take my hands off my situation and allow God to fight my battles, and herein I received the victories. Glory to God!

I never knew how God was going to help me face tomorrow *today* because I was so hurt about my setback, but I had peace knowing that He was in control of my life and my situation.

In 2021, during the pandemic season, God was still blessing my hands and my household. My publishing company, AGD Publishing, became a #1 International Company and Bestselling Company after the release of my first visionary author book through AGD Publishing. I was blessed through my publishing company to publish four authors during the pandemic season.

I AM HER! I am HEALED! I am that woman who God spoke to. During my first sermon at my home church, I preached "I am Her," from Luke 8:43-48 KJV.

> "And a woman having an issue of blood twelve years, which had spent all her living upon physicians, neither could be healed of any, came behind him, and touched the border of his garment: and immediately her issue of blood stanched. And Jesus said, "Who touched me?" When all denied, Peter and they that were with him said, "Master, the multitude throng thee and press thee, and sayest thou, 'Who touched

me?'" And Jesus said, "Somebody hath touched me: for I perceive that virtue is gone out of me." And when the woman saw that she was not hid, she came trembling, and falling down before him, she declared unto him before all the people for what cause she had touched him, and how she was healed immediately. And he said unto her, "Daughter, be of good comfort: thy faith hath made thee whole; go in peace."

I remember speaking to myself in the midnight hour that I'm going to keep pressing my way through it all; I'm going to keep soaring, I'm going to keep making a difference no matter what it takes because I am healed, I am delivered, and I have been set free. So, every day I would write in my daily journal the affirmations Holy Spirit breathed within me, and therein the vision God gave me for my life.

Protection: I read the Book of Psalms every day, but the Scripture which stood out to me the most was Psalms 91:1-4: "He that dwelleth in the secret place of the most High shall abide under the shadow of the Almighty. I will say of the LORD, He is my refuge and my fortress: my God; in him will I trust. Surely he shall deliver thee from the snare of the fowler, and from the noisome pestilence."

Mind: I realize the importance of renewing the mind, especially in challenging situations. God directed me to Romans 12:2, "And be not conformed to this world: but be ye transformed by the renewing of your mind, that ye may prove what is that good, and acceptable, and perfect, will of God."

Stand: God spoke to my heart and ministered to me the significance of making a quality decision and standing firm. GALATIANS 5:5 "Stand fast therefore in the liberty wherewith Christ hath made us free and be not entangled again with the yoke of bondage."

10 Points to Encourage Yourself

1. Step out of your comfort zone and live.

2. Live, love, and laugh more each day.

3. Enlarge your visions, your dreams, and your desires.

4. Change your perspective on how you see things.

5. Create a balance in your life and do it on purpose; live life stress-free.

6. Center yourself around positive people and people who care about you.

7. Be flexible and quick to adapt to new positive and faith-like changes.

8. Speak positive words about yourself --to yourself every day.

9. Break down or tear down the strongholds that are keeping you bound.

10. Let go of the negative and let God's Word heal you.

BREAKING THE CURSE OF HIS NURTURE

SHANIA ELLIOTT-MCDOWELL

It was February 2010, less than two weeks until my very first food tasting. I was so excited because my parents were going to be there. Who knew that this was going to be the best and worst week of my life? It was Wednesday morning. In the middle of preparing everything, my mother called, "Shania, your father is in the hospital." I immediately hung up and called my dad.

"I'll be okay," he said.

"Dad, I can cancel my tasting and go back to New York to be there with you."

"No! You need to continue with your plans and do the tasting. That was the thing I was most excited about doing when I come Charlotte, besides seeing the sights," he said with a soft chuckle.

"Dad, you can't come down here until you get healthy. How about I come up there and cook for you?" Our conversation went on for about forty-five minutes. We both said, "I love you," and hung up the phone.

Later on that night, as I was working on my menu, the phone rang. Somehow, I sensed something was wrong. "Hello."

All I heard was my mother screaming, "The nurses found your father on the floor. He had a massive heart attack." Her muffled cries were loud.

Tears streamed down my face. How could this be? We just got off the phone earlier, and now my father is gone.

Growing up, my dad was everything to me. He made sure that every day I woke up, I never wanted for anything. We had daddy-daughter dates practically every weekend—we would go to the park so I could ride my bike. In my eyes, there was nothing he could do wrong, even when we would go to a lady's house who he called, my aunt. I knew she wasn't my aunt, but someone he was seeing. It hurt that I couldn't tell my mom, but I didn't know what my dad would do. So, I watched my mother live this way as far back as I can remember. I made a promise I would not allow myself to be subjected to this or, even worse, become my father.

One Saturday morning, I can remember waking up early. I could hear, "My Girl," by the Temptations playing on the radio. Then my father yelled my name, "Shania." I was excited because I knew what was coming next, me standing on his feet, dancing in the living room. That song would play and at least three more songs before my mother would say, "Go clean your room." My dad would make my favorite hot cereal. So, I would hurry and clean up and get dressed, so I would be ready for my day with my dad.

We would start at the park. He would let me play and run and act silly with my friends. Afterward, he would go get my bike, and then we were off on our dad and daughter adventure. Those days were the most fun because we would start in the morning and come home by the time it was getting dark. Normally, we would go to my aunt's house, and I would see my older cousins and play with them for a little while. Then we would grab something to eat on the way back home. We did this almost every other weekend until I found something else I wanted to do.

I loved watching Fame and Debbie Allen on TV. After watching the show, I told my dad I wanted to be a ballet star. So, he did what only my dad would and enrolled me into a tap and ballet class. I would get up early every Saturday morning, and he would walk me to Atlantic Ave. in Brooklyn to go tap and ballet for about an hour. I enjoyed this class until the teacher said we had to do a recital. The fear that swiftly enveloped me ended my quest to become a ballet star real quick. My dad didn't mind because I was his little girl.

I never questioned my father about what he did, not only because I feared him, but back then my parents raised us to stay in a child's place. But one time I asked because I was just curious. I was about eight or nine years old and my mom, my dad, and I were sitting at the table eating breakfast. I looked at my father's arm. I said I wish my veins looked like his so the doctor could stick me better. We laughed at it, but the look my mother gave my father was a look of hurt. It wasn't the first time she looked at him like that, and it would not be the last.

My dad had a mean streak whenever he drank. He would argue with my mom and then blackout. One day we went to my aunt's house for a cookout. My mother's family didn't care for my dad, but I don't think he cared. Well, everyone was enjoying themselves. My dad showed up and made a scene. It embarrassed my mom. On the way home, I could feel my mom preparing herself for what was about to come. My dad would normally sit in his chair drinking and wait for my mom to come home. As soon as she walked through the door, it would become a verbal war of words.

Anyway, we got home, and my father sat outside with a beer in his hand. We walked inside, and he followed behind us. I could tell my mom was nervous. She gripped my hand as tight as she could while we quickly went upstairs. I was so scared every time they got into an argument because I worried that this would be the time he would kill my mom.

My dad came bounding up the stairs behind us, calling my mom every name in the book. My mother ran into the bathroom. He pushed the door open and stopped abruptly. He was shocked to see me standing in front of my mom holding a butter knife. He stared down at me, and I looked up at him. My eyes were blinking rapidly, and my hand was shaking uncontrollably. The plan wasn't to cut him. I just wanted him to stop hurting my mom. He smiled at me, nodded his head, and backed out of the bathroom. That was the last time he tried to hit my mom.

It was the beginning of my teenage years. I was turning fourteen in a couple of weeks. My mother had gotten a nasty cough. I remember my father taking her to the emergency room and returning without her. He told me she had pneumonia, so she had to stay in the hospital for a while. Every day I would watch my dad sit at the table looking worried. This scared me. I knew his nerves were getting to him.

Dad would smile and make small talk to pass the time. Then, we would cook everything, from spaghetti to fried chicken. We were enjoying our father-daughter time. I think he was trying not to make me worry.

I didn't know there was a big storm that was about to come and hit my household. Normally after school, I would go see my mom at the hospital, but on this day, I got there late. My mom and her friend were in the room talking, and my mom was in tears. I could barely hear her muffled voice. So, I moved closer to the corner of the door and heard her say "HIV" and my "father's name." It confused me because the next thing she said was she did not want to tell me, but she had already told my sister.

I heard the hurt and pain in my mother's voice; I saw her tears. My heart dropped to the floor. I didn't know what to do. Should I go in and tell her I heard everything? Why would she keep this from me? With tears streaming down my face, I ran out of the hospital. I didn't know where I wanted to go, but I knew I had to get far from there.

I hopped on the number three train and rode through Brooklyn the whole night as I tried to sort through everything. Was my mom going to die? Who was going to take care of me? Who gave my mother HIV? Had she been cheating on my father? I had so many questions, but first I needed to clear my head.

When my birthday came around, I made the best of it by thanking God for bringing my mother home safely. She put all her different medications on the table, telling me they were antibiotics for her to continue fighting off pneumonia.

"Yeah, whatever," I said, and closed myself in my room for the rest of the day.

Days passed in the house and there wasn't much talking. Occasionally, my mom gave my dad a look of evil disdain. The conversations between them were one word, if that. Mom even had a painful look on her face whenever she called his name.

During the summer of 1992, things were so different. Mom went back to babysitting her foster children, and my dad went back to work and doing side jobs. I had my first summer job as well, so I was excited to be away from the house for at least eight hours. It was at night when I hated being home.

One day, I came home a little earlier from work, and my dad was in the hallway with someone. They were busy doing *"whatever,"* that he didn't hear me come up the stairs. What I saw changed how I looked at my dad. He was kissing another woman. I was shocked! From that day forward, things were completely different between him and me.

"What's going on between you and your dad?" mom asked.

"Nothing!" I couldn't tell her the truth because I knew it would hurt her. Things stayed tense with my dad for a long time.

That September 1992, I was so excited to be in high school. I enjoyed the first few years, but, while everyone was preparing for their senior year, I didn't care about school, home, or anything else.

One night I came home past my curfew. Unfortunately, my dad and I got into a huge fight that led to a fist being thrown. So, my mom decided it would be better if I went to stay with my sister in Poughkeepsie, NY.

It was 1995, and one of my sister's friends gave me a ticket to Culinary School. They were having a presentation and a school tour. Wondering why she gave me the ticket, I debated if I was even going to go. I went anyway and saw the biggest kitchen I had ever seen. I fell in love. I didn't tell anyone, but something was telling me the kitchen was where I needed to be. After that tour, I thought I knew what I was going to do with my life, but things were about to go from bad to worse.

It took me a couple of years to realize that I was in a family full of liars. My mother took me to therapy to sit down with my father to see what was going on between us. We were getting ready to go to our first session, when my dad announced he wasn't going. He said he didn't want to tell a therapist his business. Honestly, I didn't want him to come because I needed to get information from my mom.

When we arrived at the therapist's office, the counselor introducing herself to me, "Hello Shania. I am Dr. Reid. Do you know why your mother brought you here?"

I explained why I thought we were there.

The therapist stated, "Some of that is correct." She then told me other things we would be talking about, but I didn't care about those other things.

During the session, my mom said, "Shania, why are you acting out?"

I couldn't believe her! Not once did she say, *Oh, by the way, I am HIV positive.* I was so frustrated and blurted out, "Why have you lied to me for the past few years?"

My mom looked at me perplexed.

"Don't look shocked now! How have you been living with HIV and cheating on my dad?"

My mom stopped me mid-sentence, "So, you think *I* was cheating on your dad? Well, Shania, it was your dad who gave me HIV."

"WAIT!! WHAT?? MY DAD?" This couldn't be. This man always told me about character and honesty. I was so furious I didn't even notice my mom was crying.

After that session, I fell into a deep, dark space, struggling to figure out what had just happened, and what I had heard. Revealing this to my friends was out of the question because I couldn't bare the thought of them judging my parents just because they had HIV. I didn't want to answer questions about my mom, and especially not about my father.

In January 1996, I moved back home. Things still weren't that great with my father, but I had to try for my mother's sake. I tried my best, but my father continued being upset with me like I had done something to him. So, I thought to myself, "why not really piss him off."

Eventually, I found the perfect way to upset my dad—his name was Richard. He was fifteen years older than me, and my father despised our relationship. But our romance was everything I thought true love was supposed to be, but I was only seventeen. What did I know?

Several months later, I went to the doctor. "You're pregnant!" the doctor said.

"OMG," I gasped. I was four months. In October 1997, my first son arrived. After having my son, my relationship with my dad actually became better because Richard and I had stopped dealing with each other.

Things were going well for me and my son. I was handling being a single mom, and my relationship with my dad was slowly getting back to how it used to be. We started going back into the kitchen and enjoying cooking together. Then it happened. I got pregnant again. This time I hid it from everyone because I didn't want to hear anything negative. I delivered my second son in October 1998. Now, I was a single mother with two boys. I didn't want to be a burden to my parents, so I moved back to Poughkeepsie, New York, where my sister lived.

My dad would come upstate to see us every weekend, or as often as he could. One day, I told him that being a single parent was very hard, but I was doing the best I could.

My dad said, "Shania, when the time is right, you will meet that special person."

In 1999, I thought I had found the man of my dreams. So, I married him at the end of November in 2000. A year later in 2001, I decided I needed to improve my life for my new family. So, I was off to start a new journey in the United States Army. I was excited, yet nervous. After the first month in basic training, time went by fast. My family came down for my graduation, and for the first time in years, my dad said he was proud of me.

While I was in the military, the years flew by. In 2003, my family grew larger when I had my daughter. She was born with a lot of medical issues. Every day, my dad made sure he was at the hospital with me. As my daughter was going through all her different surgeries, my husband and I were drifting apart. We ended up separating.

I moved back home in 2006, which was a bad idea. My father was getting sick, and I was on a downward spiral. I was going through a divorce and was a single mom again, this time with three children. I was lonely and got into another relationship that ended as quickly as it started.

My mother and father didn't care for the guy. What they didn't know was that he was abusing me. I hid it from my kids and parents until one day I couldn't. I don't remember what happened that day, except I had a black eye, fractured jaw, and broken nose.

Then, in 2007 my divorce was final, I moved my family to Charlotte NC, and enrolled in a culinary school. I completed my associate degree in 2008, and that summer, I met my current husband, Steven.

I decided it was time to start my private chef business, so I created "Decadent Chef."

It was now 2010, and I was planning my first culinary tasting. I was excited about this because it would be the very first time I would cook professionally for my parents. My dad would tell me all the time that he has always been proud of me, which made me smile inside. Then, two weeks before my tasting, my dad was placed in the hospital. I was going to cancel, but my father told me to go forward with my plans, so I did. We said our usual "Love you's" and hung up.

Later on that night, as I was working on my menu, the phone rang. Somehow, I knew something was wrong. It was my mother— all I heard was her screaming. She said something about the nurses found him on the floor and that he had a fatal heart attack.

The tears started streaming down my face. How could this be? We had just gotten off the phone earlier, and now he is no longer here. My entire world came crashing down.

A few days later, I had to muster up the courage to attend my father's funeral. It was so hard seeing him lying in a casket. Looking at my dad, I was reminded of the promise I made him to pursue my dream of becoming a chef and doing my tasting. But I can't do this without him.

After my dad passed, I felt empty inside. I missed him so much. My desire to cook wasn't there anymore, so "Decadent Chef" was no longer.

From 2011 to 2019, I went through trying to figure out what to do with my life. I just didn't have the energy to walk into a kitchen— mostly out of fear of failing. Not being able to have that one person who would cheer me on scared me.

In March of 2012, Steve and I got married, and I thought everything was going well. Then, we lost his dad the following month. It was one of the hardest times, at least that's what we thought.

We had started the IVF process to have another child, and in 2014 we found out we were pregnant. May 2015 was supposed to be our happy month, but two weeks before our son was born, Steve's mother passed. The death of his mother sent him into a state of deep grief.

After that, we struggled as a married couple. I fell into postpartum depression for almost two years—this caused me to seek what I thought was love from someone else. This sent my marriage into turmoil. By the time 2019 hit, I was in the lowest place that I could ever be. We were going through a pandemic, my marriage was in shambles, my mother contracted Covid, and we were trying to get past my husband's depression and my infidelity. This dark space had my mind all over the place.

Then, I met a woman who helped me get my light back. She turned what I thought was over, into something I could get excited about again. One Friday night in 2020, I was dreaming about a mirror in a room. In the reflection was a man who looked like my father and a little girl who looked like me. This man told the little girl, "It's okay to start over. I will always be here with you." I woke up in a sweat, and tears began to fall.

The next Sunday at church I made the decision to get baptized and to give my life to Christ. It gave me the faith to relaunch "Decadent Chef." I also started my nonprofit, Happiness Is Vibrant, to assist people with autoimmune diseases to learn how to eat correctly while taking their medication. As my life continues to evolve, I believe the apple does fall from the same tree but has the ability to form its own roots.

"To fully accept your calling, you have to resolve where you come from." Chandler Moore

FROM THE GHETTO TO THE GOLF COURSE

CHARLES G KEARSE

"Where there is no vision, the people perish: but he that keepeth the law, happy is he."

(Proverbs 29:18 King James Version)

"I have a dream today! I have a dream that one day every valley shall be exalted, and every hill and mountain shall be made low. The rough places will be plain, and the crooked places will be made straight, and the glory of the Lord shall be revealed, and all flesh shall see it together. This is our hope." Dr. Martin Luther King Jr.

"When the dream is big enough, your current conditions don't matter." Charles G. Kearse

My story is a story of redemption.

Arrested by God

The movie, *Brooklyn's Finest* and the Mike Tyson documentary, *The Knockout*, capture the essence of my early teenage years. The lives of many Black boys being raised by single moms are filled with hopelessness and uncertainty. Many single moms, like my mother, do a

78

great job of loving their boys. Unfortunately, they are ill-equipped to raise men while fighting against the powerful streets that make their mark on the curious male mind. The lure of sex, money, and drugs can easily capture the imagination of Black boys and teens. Often their fathers are not there to guide them from the pitfalls of the ghetto.

I grew up in a loving, dysfunctional environment in the neighborhood of Brooklyn, New York, called Brownsville. Brownsville is known for its high crime rate. Growing up, in order to survive the streets, I had to fight bigger, older kids who had cycled in and out of jail and detention centers. These kids were repeatedly caught committing petty crimes that led down the road to long-term incarceration or death. The only difference between my friends and me was that by the grace of God, I didn't get caught. Instead, I was arrested by God.

My memory of my earlier childhood days is filled with lots of fun and laughter. We spent a lot of time playing in the neighborhood with people of all different backgrounds. Growing up in Brownsville was fun because of the neighborhood's diversity. We spent a lot of time around our family. My mother had eleven brothers and sisters, each with an average of two children. So, I have a ton of cousins scattered all over the five boroughs of New York City. We'd travel to my family members' homes almost every week. Most lived in the "projects" or in apartments in the Bedford Stuyvesant neighborhood of Brooklyn; only a few family members were homeowners. They say it takes a village to raise a child, and I was surrounded by a beautiful, loving one.

I will never forget when my Aunt Linda got married and her new husband, Arnold, moved her and her two children into their own beautiful, brick brownstone. Their home became the go-to spot for our family celebrations. Their home was warm and welcoming. My

79

new uncle owned a BBQ restaurant right around the corner. This gave me the opportunity to have an authentic look at what owning a thriving business was like.

Aunt Linda and Uncle Arnold weren't the only homeowners in the family. My Uncle Johnny owned his home on Long Island, and my Aunt Pat owned a condo in Harlem, both of whom played important roles in my upbringing. They taught me the importance of owning real estate. I believe that owning a home is one of the keys to creating generational wealth.

My mom, my brother, and I moved a few times in my childhood before landing in Brownsville. While it was an affordable housing option, it was also a neighborhood filled with many obstacles to overcome. As a boy growing up in Brownsville, I got swept up in the culture of the streets. Without a father to lead me into becoming a man, I ended up taking guidance from the wrong crowd.

I met my father twice in my entire life. The first time I met him, I was five years old when my mother took me to meet him on his bookie route—he was known to run in the Brooklyn gambling scene. I was thirty-two the second time I saw him. I caught up with my father on his bookie route again, hoping to make arrangements for him to meet his grandchildren. We spoke briefly, and it was clear he wasn't doing well. Riddled with ailments, he was in the midst of preparing for surgery and a hospital stay.

As my father stood in front of me, I saw what my life could've been like if not for God's hand. I told my father I had forgiven him. After saying goodbye, he promised to reach out to plan a meeting with my son and daughter. I had hoped in my heart we would meet again, and that my children could meet him. But to this day, he still has not met his grandchildren. I carry no grudge or negative thoughts towards my father. Instead, I strive to use his failure to father me as a concrete lesson.

God gave me the opportunity to be the father I never had. Boys and girls need to know how to navigate life's paths to achieve their potential. I believe the broken conditions of families are one of the reasons we are plagued with poverty. Poverty in America leads to trying to make it at any cost. A "get rich or die trying" attitude causes many young African American boys to resort to crime to try to help their struggling families.

I flirted with the "thug life" because I wanted to help my mom put food on the table. I didn't like seeing Mom having to work menial jobs to take care of my brother and me. She was always a hard worker and tried to give us more than she had. She successfully gave love and life's necessities, but I wanted more, and I went about getting it the wrong way.

By the Grace of God

My life was saved as I was robbing a man in the hallway of the Van Dyke Houses, located at Livonia Ave and Stone Ave. The hallways of the project were always infested with thugs, just like me, who risked being arrested or killed in a scuffle. My move was the sleeper hold. I knew it well, and once the man was unconscious, I could steal whatever valuables he had with him.

However, one day, God interrupted my plans. I heard the strong and real voice of God, my new Father. His voice stopped me in my tracks and told me, "There's a better way!" Everything I needed, every void I yearned to be filled, was all in Him and his promise. I gave my heart to the Lord. I knew things would be different, not only for the man who was exceptionally grateful that I hadn't hurt him, but for my life, my soul, and for all of the people I could lead to the

Lord. I felt an unexplainable sense of peace, and I couldn't wait to spread it to others.

As I got older, God continued to reveal Himself to me through the Holy Spirit and the Bible. I finally began to dream of a better future for my life. Like the other boys growing up in the ghetto, I started to dream of getting out by becoming an athlete.

Football was my game, and I played with strength and passion. I hadn't played many sports due to chronic asthma and a severe heart murmur. Playing with the rest of the boys would often land me in the hospital, with my Mom by my side, assuring me that I would be okay. I spent so much time in the hospital that I wanted to become a doctor. I wanted to help patients heal and be whole. Asthma and a heart murmur were a threat to me if I wanted to be the athlete I knew I needed to be.

I read in the Bible how Jesus healed people who discovered His promise in 1 Peter 2:24, "Who his own self bare our sins in his own body on the tree, that we, being dead to sins, should live unto righteousness: by whose stripes ye were healed." I received supernatural healing and restoration in my body. I was able to pursue my dream of becoming a football player.

After God saved me, I knew I had to change my environment if I was ever going to be able to bring about change in my environment. Oftentimes, God must deliver a leader *of* the people that he may present a leader *to* the people. I had to get out of Brownsville or transfer high schools in the eleventh grade so I could play one year of high school football in my senior year.

Football and getting good grades became my ticket out of the ghetto. I went to American International College (AIC) with a scholarship and financial aid package. My days at AIC were filled with excitement and adventure. I was surrounded by a diverse student body, and I was able to continue teaching my friends and peers about the promise of God.

As a first-generation college student, I had no clue how to navigate college. It took me attending two different universities to finally receive my Bachelor of Arts and Master of Business Administration degrees, while serving in the military. I used to dream of becoming a medical doctor, but I'm living my deferred dream of earning my Ph.D. I still dream of helping and healing sick people, but my focus is now on economic healing.

Part of my college journey led me to the University of Tulsa, where I was exposed to the Greenwood community located in North Tulsa. I was able to apply my love of the Lord and explore my destiny of teaching God's Word with like-minded people.

Through my life experiences, I learned early on that everything rises and falls, based on leadership–good or bad. We sure had unlimited access to bad leaders in our community. Harvard University research states that when a community doesn't have access to credible leadership, it will suffer the disparities that inner cities are plagued with. Situations like mine are the reason most of my Black and Latino friends got caught up in the streets and went straight into the prison pipeline.

This chapter is too short for me to tell how God has fulfilled his promise to me. I will simply say, "God is Good!" For forty-seven years, I have experienced God's love, grace, protection, provision, and fellowship. Though it has not been an easy road, He has led and guided me through the good, the bad, and the ugly. I'm currently living out the dream of empowering people to win through the Gospel and entrepreneurship. As a trainer and coach, I'm helping people discover their dreams of business or ministry leadership. My company helps people put sample strategies and systems in place to live

God's *better way* for their lives. You will always have two choices in life–your way or God's way. I implore you to choose God's way. It will lead you to the abundance of life that Jesus has promised.

"I call heaven and earth to record this day against you, that I have set before you life and death, blessing and cursing: therefore choose life, that both thou and thy seed may live" (Deuteronomy 30:19).

As a visionary and entrepreneurial leader, I have lost some of the most important relationships of my life as I pursue God's dreams. But I have held onto the dreams that God has put in my heart. Many of those dreams, which once were deferred, are now coming to pass.

Able To Do Far More Abundantly Beyond All That We Ask or Think

Since my days of escaping the negative influences of the thug life-style, I learned the art of "solo exploration." Taking time away from people allowed me to strengthen my relationship and bond with the Lord. Through solo exploration, we can hear and feel God's guidance. His voice is the loudest of them all, but time alone makes it that much clearer. I often still find myself working alone, talking with God, dreaming of a better day. You would be amazed at what dreams God will drop in your heart while spending time with Him.

I have had many of my dreams come to pass, from earning my undergraduate and graduate degrees, to planting life-giving churches, to international travel, to flying in private jets and helicopters, to living in million-dollar homes and driving fancy cars. God sure has been good to this Black boy from Brooklyn.

Pathways to Victory Is My Dream Deferred

There is one more dream God placed in my heart over two decades ago. I believe God spoke to me and said football was my ticket out of the ghetto, but golf would be my passport to the world. I believe golf can be used as an instrument of change. Although the dream is deferred, the dream is alive!

"And he said unto them, 'Go ye into all the world, and preach the gospel to every creature'" (Mark 16:15).

I have created a golf business that serves an $84 billion-dollar industry. This business is the building block outlined in Nehemiah 2:18, "And they said, 'Let us rise up and build.' So, they strengthened their hands for this good work."

We are rising up and rebuilding Black Wall Street all over America and the world. I believe God has put this dream in my heart for the second half of my life.

To my co-authors, God is calling us to lead the charge. You cannot quit, no matter how hard the journey is. We must rise and build. Remember, quitters never win. Winners never quit.

Words to Win By

My mission in life is to empower you to win. We win by the Word of God. As a teacher of the Word, a trainer, and a business coach, I want to give you some words so you can win in your business.

Deuteronomy 8:18 says, "But remember the LORD your God, for it is he who gives you the ability to produce wealth."

All of the skills and special talents we use in our businesses are all given to us by God. He gives us the ability to make money and close deals. He did it for our parents, our mentors, and he does it for us too.

The Bible commands us to be innovative in our businesses. We should not ever try to be like anyone else. The world is always waiting for the next, best thing. We must renew ourselves by being lifelong learners and reading constantly. It is important to have a prayerful life as an entrepreneur, as it helps you on those days when things do not go your way. You need to have the strength to thank God, even when you do not close that big deal. God protects us when we do not get opportunities we think we can't survive without. His plan is what matters, above all else!

Always be honest and humble. Do not be afraid to tell clients or employees that you do not know the answer. Try to diffuse any issues with truth and take full responsibility for fixing the problem. Never let your ego get in the way of doing what's in the best interest of your business. God always delivers to us what we need in order to do our best work. Sometimes he sends a check we need just in time, and other times he sends us creativity to find the best solution to our challenges. Trust in the Lord at all times. Always be grateful.

Fear is the enemy of entrepreneurship. God wants us to take advantage of the power he gives us to pursue our ideas. However, we must use our power wisely and not put all of our hard work at risk by not being focused on our small *and* large goals. You must be fiscally disciplined in business. It is painful at times, but it will produce quite a harvest. Running a business is hard. It's a marathon, not a sprint. There will be plenty of stumbling blocks in your way. Everyone trips and falls while running this race, but winners get up faster than everyone else. You must do what you need to do to win your race.

There will be times when you are the only person who believes in your dream. Don't be afraid. Believe in yourself and your business idea. You must be willing to make tough decisions in your small business. No one else will do it for you. Remember, you'll always have

God as your guide. Make hard decisions quickly and often, so you can move on to doing the work needed to help your clients.

Proverbs 11:14 says, "Without the guidance of good leaders a nation falls. But many good advisers can save it."

It is critical to have a "cabinet" of advisors for your small business–people who have different strengths and knowledge which complement your vision. Your business will not survive on your experience alone. Pull together a group of people who are invested in your success. The group should include an existing entrepreneur, a customer, a mentor, a lawyer, and an accountant. Seek out a mastermind group or peer-to-peer mentoring program to help as well.

"I can do all things through Christ who strengthens me" (Philippians 4:13).

Whenever you struggle with your self-confidence, read this bible verse to yourself. There will be times in your business when you need to force yourself to stretch beyond what you think is possible. You can do it! You must do what God has put in your heart. I believe in you.

The Birth of a Movement and Its Simple Process

I am on a mission to birth a movement that empowers "members of socially and economically disenfranchised communities" to change their lives, economic status, and worldview, thereby changing communities through the love of God, servant leadership, and entrepreneurship. Therefore, I created The Urban Impact Movement to Raise a Tribe of Urban Impact Entrepreneurs to Transform Urban Inner Cities Worldwide.

The Pathway to Victory Movement is a simple process that the lowest level participant can implement. We have chosen the baseball diamond to illustrate the movement process. Our first, second, and third bases are progressive measurements of individual and corporate growth. The home plate is both the starting place and the scoring point in our approach. At any time, we will be able to measure how many people are engaged in the movement, how many people have scored, and how many people are on deck, ready to enter the. We will focus on the part that needs a boost to maintain the momentum of the "game" moving forward to achieve the mission–Empowering Disenfranchised Communities to take control of their destinies.

"Our approach to community development and engagement is not just telling people what to do but bringing them along so they can understand what's required of them to control their environment, their own space, their building, and their future."

Ibon Muhammad, Director of Special Projects, Fifth Avenue Committee

The Urban Impact Movement is challenging to pursue, but when we are successful, its benefits will impact not only the entrepreneurs who succeed but also society. Disenfranchised communities will be transformed and enjoy both stronger economies and a new breed of leaders—ones capable of effecting change in the community and society at large. Private-sector corporations will benefit from more dependable suppliers and contractors, taking on significant opportunities and eventually fostering minority business programs of their own. These businesses will contribute to the government's economic development plan—revitalizing inner-city communities, expanding the tax base, and creating new jobs.

An important part of the movement will be the BH365 Cafe. The cafe focuses on the inner city/urban markets and provides events such as spoken word, jazz night, a gospel brunch, and Latin band night. BH365 Cafe fulfills its socioeconomic mission by providing resources and opportunities for inner-city residents.

The BH365 Cafe is a part of a comprehensive strategy for customers to support and stabilize urban/inner-city communities by donating a percentage of pre-tax profits to inner-city youth sports, creating clusters of businesses and community organizations to help promote homeownership, community investment, entrepreneurship, and accountability. The goal is to help communities recycle dollars earned within their neighborhoods for an extended period, creating a more economically viable community.

The Urban Impact Movement has partnered with Black History 365®, a comprehensive curriculum designed for public schools across America. Our purpose is to provide a tech-savvy educational resource that will invite students, educators, and others to become:

- critical thinkers

- compassionate listeners

- fact-based, respectful communicators

- action-oriented solutionists.

I invite you to become a part of the movement.

RISING BEYOND THE VEIL

VERN HAMIL

As a young child growing up in St. Mary, Jamaica, I always knew I was destined for greatness; however, how I was going to achieve this was not clear. As I became older, I realized the events which took me from one place to another would eventually shape my destiny.

I had just turned sixteen, when I was invited to a sweet sixteen birthday party in Kingston, Jamaica. My grandmother thought it over for weeks before she told Clara K, who was hosting the party for her daughter, Kandy C, that she would allow me to go. I was so excited since I had never been to a party or anyone's house for a weekend before.

We arrived at the house in Kingston, Clara K showed me to my room, and I unpacked my bags. I looked at my night gown that my mom had sent from London and held it close to my chest. The sweet smell of lavender perfume came from the fabric. I was tired but couldn't sleep. This was too much for me. I couldn't believe I was in Kingston to attend a real party and stay over the weekend.

On the day of the party, the living room was decorated so beautifully with balloons. There was a bar to the far right, and the DJ played music outside on the verandah. My role was to meet and greet the guest. So, I got dressed and put on my best smile. I was ready for the night, but I was not ready for what the night had in store for me.

The party was a blast, and everyone had a good time. I was complimented on my hair and my smile. Every time I went to the bar, I had tonic water. In the wee hours when the party was winding down, I went to the bar and got my drink. As I stepped away, someone called my name. I turned around, and there stood Roy grinning at me with that smile. Roy was our school bus driver who had developed a reputation of being very promiscuous with the schoolgirls and even getting some of them pregnant. I had a conversation with him once, inquiring if all the rumors about him were true. He never gave me a clear response.

"You look so good. Come and have a drink with me," he said.

"Thanks, but I can't." I said and just walked away as he stared at me. We had never even had another conversation after I had asked him about the other girls. So, I couldn't understand why he was asking me to have a drink with him. I walked back to where the girls were and engaged in a conversation they were having about the cute boys at their school.

When the party was over, I retired to my bedroom. Shortly after, I was awakened by a knock on the door. It was Clara K.

"Roy wants to talk to you," she said.

I thought it was strange that he wanted to talk to me at that time of the night. But I got out of bed, still in my nightgown, and followed her to the front door. Clara K opened the door and tilted her head towards Roy's direction where he sat drinking a Red Stripe beer. I heard the door close behind me.

"What?" I asked, feeling annoyed.

"Sit," he said, "I want to talk to you."

Reluctantly, I sat in the chair beside him.

"My friends were inquiring about you, and I told them you were my girlfriend, he said.

Stunned by his statement, I asked, "How old are you? Furthermore, I have a boyfriend," I lied. The moment those words left my lips I regretted them. I could tell my answer caught him by surprise.

"Really?" he inquired.

Before I could answer and correct myself, he changed the subject.

"Let's go talk in the car; I want to show you something," he said.

"We can talk tomorrow. I am very tired and need to go back to bed, I told him.

However, he insisted on showing me something in his car. So, I reluctantly walked with him to the car and sat in the passenger seat. He turned on the radio and I began to relax as I listened to the music. Suddenly, he drove off. Startled, I quickly sat upright in my seat.

"I am going to show you some great scenery and the city below."

My heart sank. This was not good. "Please, take me back," I pleaded, but he just kept driving. Then, he abruptly stopped and turned the car engine off. All of a sudden, he was like a wild animal ripping off my nightgown.

I screamed, "Stop! Stop! No! No!" I tried hitting him in the face, but he was too strong for me. This punk is going to rape me! All I could think of was how much I loathed him. He entered me with such force that all I could do was scream as tears ran down my face. He took control of my body. It seemed like an eternity, but then he climaxed and stopped abruptly.

Suddenly, there was a loud knock on the car window. As I looked up, I saw a cop standing there who asked him to step outside. When the Officer interrogated him, he told him that I was his girlfriend and had my permission.

"We were just having rough sex, Officer," he said. Look, she is in her night gown." The Officer took his word for it, and I watched in horror as he just walked away.

To this day, I do not understand why I didn't stand up to him. I blame myself for not telling the Officer the truth, but I guess I was in shock. I was so devastated and tried to comprehend the gravity of what really happened. I was so distraught and frightened. I cried all the way back to the house. He opened the door, and I somehow stumbled to the room I was staying in.

I saw my reflection in the mirror, but didn't recognize the stranger staring back at me. I looked at my ripped nightgown stained with blood. I curled up in a fetal position on the floor and wept.

Someone knocked and the door opened. It was Clara K.

"What the heck happened to you?" she asked, as she dropped to the floor beside me and began rocking me back and forth. I held my face up and stared at her as hot, burning tears streaming down my face.

"How could you do this to me? Why did you wake me up and send me out to him? You were supposed to protect me," I sobbed. She took me to the bathroom, and I stood under the shower trying to scrub the dirt and slime off my body. Maybe all this was a bad dream, and I was going to wake up from it. I lay down and cried myself to sleep that night.

The next day I stayed in bed; I didn't want to eat or drink anything. I just wanted to die. Roy came to see me later that day. "I am so sorry," he said, "I didn't know you were a virgin. You told me you had a boyfriend. The truth is, I had fallen in love with you."

I glared at him with contempt and disgust. "Why are you here? To rape me again? I will make it easier for you this time," I said. I got off the bed and started removing my clothes. He got up and walked away.

I was still in disbelief. I did not move in his circle. The high school girls he ran around with were not even my friends, and I was never friendly with him. So how could I end up being a statistic?

The shame, the guilt, the regret of not being able to defend myself against this beast washed over me once more. I turned my head to the wall and started sobbing. Then out of nowhere, my entire body started to shake. "Oh God, no. Please, dear God, don't let me die without seeing Ma B, my grandmother. I am going to die." These were all the things that raced through my mind at that moment.

I hadn't eaten all day, so I felt weak and nauseous. I thought maybe I was dehydrated and was about to faint. I sat there in a daze, motionless and scared. What if I never saw my grandmother again? "Oh, Ma B, where are you?" I whispered in the darkness of the room. Finally, the shaking subsided, but my hands were still visibly shaking.

Clara K walked into the room with food and drink on a tray. I held the glass to my lips, but my hands shook so badly she had to help me.

"What did he do to you?" she asked looking surprised.

"I want to go home," I said.

She wrapped her arms around me and hugged me. It felt comforting for a moment, then I lashed out again, "Take me home! I don't want to die here!"

The next morning, I was supposed to dress in uniform for school, and then stop by my house, drop my bag off, then continue to school. Instead, I just dressed in the same clothes I wore that Friday.

"Aren't you going to school?" Clara K asked. I just looked at her in awe of her stupidity as I walked out to get on the bus.

After that, Clara K and I remained relatively cold towards each other. In my heart, I believed she betrayed me by waking me up and putting me in that situation. Although I will forever blame myself for walking and getting into the car with him, I did so because I felt comfortable at that moment in his company. I didn't like his reputation, but not in my wildest dreams could I have ever thought *that* would happen. Now, I would have to see his face almost every freaking day, and the anger began to boil within me. He was a big grown-ass man, and I was just sixteen. This was the worst thing that could ever happen. But why me?

The bus stopped at my house, and I got off. When I saw Ma B, I just wrapped my arms around her, caught up in the moment with the one I loved the most.

Even though it was years after that fateful night that I arrived in the United States to live, the pain from that traumatic experience still pierced me and kept me up at night.

Sometime later, I was diagnosed with Cervical Spinal Stenosis, the narrowing of the spinal canal, which is painful. The doctor recommended I get surgery to correct the problem. However, I opted for a second opinion which stressed physical therapy and epidural injections to try and delay the inevitable.

Eventually, on January 7, 2013, I had a cervical discectomy and fusion at five levels c2 thru c7. It took me a year to recover. During that period of laying on my back, I discovered the real Christ and his unconditional love for me. I drew closer to God and began to pray more and worship more. While I was cut off from all things that didn't matter, I learned to trust him more.

Just as I was beginning to find myself, I was dealt another blow. When I returned to work, I noticed I was still having pain and discomfort. My friend, Johnny, had the same medical condition and referred me to his doctor at Lincoln Hospital in Bronx, New York. After doing a C-Scan, he discovered that the pins at two levels were not anchored to the bones. So, in June of 2014, five months after returning to work, I had to do a revision surgery to correct the problem. I was out of work for another six months.

Finally, I was given my life back, and I felt so good about myself. However, this feeling was short-lived, as I noticed I wasn't as competent at my job as before. I started making simple mistakes and that became an issue with my boss, but I pressed on.

Then, in May of 2018, I woke up one morning and put my feet on the floor. Out of nowhere, pain came shooting down the back of my feet. The excruciating pain caused me to stumble back to the bed while crying my heart out. What is this now, Lord? When I regained my composure, I searched the internet for "pain running down the back of your feet," and my symptoms pointed to something called "Sciatica."

My neurosurgeon and my neurologist later confirmed that it really was Sciatica. I braced myself for the news I dreaded most. I was told I had to have another surgery to correct this condition; however, I would be able to return to work in six weeks.

In November 2018, I placed my faith in God's hands and underwent a lumbar laminectomy. During my four weeks of recovery, I noticed a big bulge on my left side. I immediately called my surgeon and went to see him. I will never forget the look on his face when he saw me. The devastating news rocked me to my core. The vertebrae had shifted. This happened with one in millions, but I just had to be the one. As I sat there and listened to the doctor explaining my present situation, I wanted to burst out in tears. The only solution would be another lumbar surgery, L4-S1 posterior fusion, with a recovery time of six to nine months.

On March 25, 2019, I did my fourth spinal surgery. I was not in a good place. My body was ravaged with muscle spasms and pain. How much more could I endure? I spent three of the most difficult weeks of my life at a hospital rehabilitation unit. At their first team meeting, the doctors told my husband they were worried about my condition and thought I might not be able to pull through. My husband told them if anyone could, it would be me, because I was strong.

In retrospect, my situation was grave. I remember my eighteen-year-old grandson came to my rehab program with me, then went home and told his mom how worried he was because I was not able to do what was required.

While in rehabilitation, I had setback after set back. I developed a condition called Meralgia Paresthetica, burning pain in the outer part of my thigh. The burning was so intense that when I screamed out in agony, all the doctors and nurses formed a line around my bed. I just could not control myself. It was my neurologist, my neurosurgeon, and the doctors at the rehab who got together and designed a treatment plan for me. Whenever the burning began, no clothing could touch the skin of the upper thigh. I thank God it was only my left thigh; I could not have survived pain in both thighs.

By the second week, I had improved tremendously. Then out of nowhere, I was told I had an E-coli infection, and as a precaution, required contact isolation. Anyone coming to see me would have to put on protective gear. My meals were left at the Nurse's Station, and then one of the nurses would suit up and bring them to me. This went on for about three to four days.

I never wavered in my faith, because by the grace of God, my work on earth was not done. God had taken me through the most trying times, and I knew he could see me through this.

During this extremely difficult time, I noticed my right hand was looking unusually different and my fingers were folding. *Oh Lord, what now?* I saw one of the doctors at Lincoln Hospital who took one look at my hand and told me it was compression from the neck. I was so disappointed to learn that this condition was associated with my prior medical situation.

I immediately went to see my neurosurgeon, who confirmed my worst fear—I needed surgery again. After I did my revision cervical surgery in 2014, my neck was holding up ok. I did not want to do another surgery on my neck, and I told him that. So, he referred me to the hand specialist, who told me if I didn't do the surgery, I could end up losing the use of my entire arm. I was devastated and distraught. I was physically drained and emotionally broken. What did I do to deserve all this?

On June 3, 2019, three months after my second lumbar surgery, I was back in Operating Room four to do my third neck surgery. The operating team all knew me by name since this was my third procedure with them. I was still recovering from my lumbar surgery, so now I had two procedures to recover from simultaneously.

Throughout this whole experience, I never gave up and fought on even when it looked like I was going to die from all the unexplained events that baffled the medical professionals taking care of me. I looked at the bigger picture of being in the arms of God, knowing no weapon formed against me would prosper.

I worked for the city of New York and was allowed to take a medical leave of absence for a year. It was approaching the one-year mark, and I was still recovering from my surgeries. I could clearly see the writing on the wall that I was going to lose my job. I wasn't ready for retirement, but I just could not return to work. I was disappointed for not being able to put myself in a better position financially, but I was relieved to hand in my retirement paperwork.

I asked myself, "What's next? I had survived, and I was going to find and live out my purpose. I drew my strength from the Creator, and I would forever be grateful for his grace to overcome. As I looked in the mirror and saw the reflection of my life, I knew God had a special plan for my life, and I also knew as a true believer, my destiny would not be reversed. My doctors always marveled at my strength and my personality. When they offered me an anti-depressant, I refused; I could deal with anything thrown at me. I read the Bible and got comforted by the Psalms of David and other scriptures. I believed the power of prayer would keep me going and forever in His grace.

I was now home. I had no job, and I was going out of mind. I was not used to this, even though I took so many medical leaves of absence. I still wanted to work and be a contributing member of society. It was then I decided to concentrate on my writing. It was my God-given talent, and I was not using it as God intended. In 2008, I had published a poetry book with Author House, but nothing happened. I sold a few copies, and that was it. However, when God has a plan for you, you just have to wait for the manifestation.

In 2018, I made contact with Joan T Randall, whom I knew from Jamaica. I was motivated by her and decided I was going to invest in myself and join her coaching program. But then I had all my medical issues and put that plan on the back burner. In 2020, I contacted her again and started listening to her Monday morning motivational at 7:30 am. I knew she was the one to get me over this hump. I used to write when I was in Jamaica and had a few articles published. However, all my life, I envisioned a writing career as a published author with recognition. I was determined to turn my dream in to reality. I took the manuscript I had in 2018, looked it over, and decided to submit it to Victorious You Press. I was told, yes, my book would be published.

On Tuesday, November 17, 2020, I launched my debut novel, "No Tears for Aiden." I finally did it! It was a long time coming, but all my pain and suffering was now paying off. Every battle fought, every trial, every heartache bought me to this moment. Finally, I am walking in my purpose.

My pastor said, "Until you say 'yes' to your purpose, your life is empty."

The satisfaction one gets from doing something they are good at and seeing the results is awesome. I was able to overcome because of God's love for me. Today, I am a bestselling author because God gave me the grace to rise up!

AFFIRMATIONS

I am selected

I am significant

I am supplied

I was created in His image and carry His DNA

I am my purpose

Write your personal affirmation/s here:

SECTION 3

DELIBERATE DAMAGE

The people that hurt us the most are the people closest to us. They often do not recognize the pain they cause because of their own brokenness. The effects of their behaviors can cause lasting damage. How does the recipient of those damages break the cycle and prevent the cyclone of similar patterns of behaviors?

"Yet, in all these things we are more than conquerors and gain an overwhelming victory through Him who loved us [so much that He died for us]." Romans 8:37 Amplified Bible

IN SEARCH OF ME: HEALED AND WHOLE

TONYA BARBEE

I remember like it was yesterday, only about six years of age, witnessing my father stab my mother repeatedly in her back while she yelled for help. My three sisters and I watched in horror as blood splattered on my grandmother's pure white walls. It was a scene I will never forget. We could have easily lost two parents that night. My grandmother went to get her black and white pistol to end my mother's abuse, but apparently, my mother wanted to save my father, despite what he did to her. So, she slapped the gun out of my grandmother's hand, which gave my father time to escape.

To this day, we do not know why my father had so much contempt for my mother that night. Being the decorated military officer that he was, he didn't serve any time. No one in my family talked about the incident again. From time to time, I just remember hearing my mother talk about getting thirty-two stitches in her back.

After that, I became obsessed with the concept of a perfect family because I knew mine was far from it. I made a vow to prove to my parents that I would do better, be better for my own family someday, and off I went trying.

My obsession for the Brady Bunch is where it began. I saw them as the perfect family. It was a sitcom of three boys with their biological dad, and three girls with their birth mom, coming together as a blended family with a maid and a cute pet. This popular show aired from 1969-1974. They managed to raise six kids all under the same roof! I figured if they could do it, why couldn't my parents? I would get home from school as fast as I could to watch this show every day. They were presented with a problem, but by the end of the episode, they had a solution. How hard was that? I was determined to find the perfect family, just like the Brady Bunch.

My parents eventually divorced, and the custody battles went on and on with my youngest sister and me. My father lived in South Carolina, my mother, in North Carolina. The back and forth was devastating. If only parents knew how much this affects the children, maybe they would be more amicable.

One night, my dad was returning me and my little sister home to my mom. My mom wasn't there to receive us at the agreed-upon time. We waited for hours, parked in front of our house, to no avail. We fell asleep waiting. Finally, at almost 11:00 pm, she pulled into the driveway, sat there for ten minutes with a man in the driver's seat, and then pulled off.

My dad asked, "What do you want to do?"

I was only eleven, but after giving it careful thought, I replied, "Daddy, I think we should stay with you."

So, my dad drove us sixty miles back to his home. The next day, he hired an attorney, and in no time, he got full custody. I will never understand why my mother left us that night, but I was happier with my dad.

I felt protected. I blocked out what he did to my mom and felt rescued that he took my little sister and me into his home.

But that feeling I had was short-lived. Dad eventually remarried. His new wife was kind at first, but that changed shortly afterward. By the time I was in the eighth grade, I had to get away from my stepmom. When she was upset with my father, she often took it out on me. I ran away from my father to live with my mother and her new husband in Washington, DC.

My mom enrolled me in middle school in DC. I felt lost. Although I reconnected with my two older sisters, I felt I betrayed my dad and left my sister behind. It was so much on me. It reminded me of my vow to create the perfect family someday.

Middle school to high school went so fast! It became my haven. I made good grades, became the drum majorette, excelled in the drama department, was inducted into the humanities program, joined a band as a singer, and made some great friends. I was finally feeling like I belonged. My baby sister eventually joined me. Then my mom left my step-dad because they often fought, and he drank too much. I was grateful I didn't have to change schools.

My mother was very resourceful. She worked as a college administrator, and we always thought she was rich because she seemed to acquire the most beautiful homes.

I met my first sweetheart who lived around the corner from us. I fell in love with him because he was kind, treated me with respect, had a car, would pick me up from school, carried my books, and took me home. He was going to be my husband. We courted our last two years in high school. I was less than six weeks pregnant when we went to the Justice of the Peace.

My mother was furious with me because I had gotten accepted at Howard University and North Carolina Central University. She said if I didn't abort, I had to leave her home. My boyfriend's family took me in until we eventually moved into our first apartment. Six months later, our bundle of joy came, a beautiful boy. By then, my mom had forgiven me and helped me to take care of him.

My husband had graduated from smoking marijuana to using other serious drugs–that became his priority. Although I tried to help him, his drug habit only got worse. I could no longer support him. Eventually, we divorced.

There goes my perfect family. I had failed. With my son in tow, I vowed to him that we would have the ideal family someday.

Years later, one of my best male friends took me out to one of the hottest clubs in Maryland. We went in like a couple, but subtly, both hoping to meet that particular person that we could potentially love. And within thirty minutes of being there, I locked eyes with a handsome man who had big eyes, was six feet tall, with a chocolate complexion, and dressed well. He was smiling at me. It was like neither of us could take our eyes off one another. My friend broke my trance and told me he was one of the judges for the live entertainment.

The smiling, handsome man walked boldly over to me, and asked me to dance. I was hooked by this charming man. I could tell he wanted me. We danced till my feet hurt. Later, he walked me to the car as my friend strolled behind us, as if offering me protection. I got in the car on the passenger side and gave him my number. He smiled at me, walked over to my friend, and gave him a manly hug as if to say, "thank you." As we pulled off, I was in a trance. I knew this would be my next husband. My family will soon be complete because my son needed a father.

In no time, he bonded with my little man. Within a year, he asked me to marry him. I gladly accepted.

I HAD MIXED FEELINGS while I walked down the aisle in my lace cream dress holding a beautiful pink and white rose bouquet in my trembling hands. I knew I should be happy, but in my heart, I felt something wasn't right. My family and coworkers were there, and they all bought us gifts. I glanced at my little man beaming from ear-to-ear. I ignored my reluctant feelings, and said, "I do."

My husband moved into my tiny apartment, and shortly afterward, my new perfect family became a rollercoaster ride before I even had a chance to put on my seatbelt. My charming husband quickly lost his charm and his job. He seemed bitter and didn't want to get another job unless it paid well. I saw his potential and encouraged him to apply for other sales jobs. Eventually, he did and began to do very well. We had our beautiful baby girl, adding to our "perfect" family. We then moved to a rental townhome.

By the time baby girl was seven, his sales career had begun to soar! I still had my stable government job. We searched for the perfect home to buy and settled on a brand-new home in a premier community. We moved in during Thanksgiving, and within twenty-four hours, I had personally unpacked each box and invited the family over for dinner even though I ordered the turkey pre-cooked. That simple act had some family members decline the invitation, but we were so proud to share our new home with the extended family on both sides.

After being promoted to an executive, my husband began to travel all over the country for his job. I was left at home to care for the kids, hold down my job, and take care of the house. Soon, I found out I was pregnant again. Depression set in because he didn't want me to have this child. I refused to do what he wanted me to do. I wanted to be strong, but I became distraught, exhausted, and burned out from my daily responsibilities with no help from him. He didn't seem to notice. We grew further apart. His boss recommended he move to the west coast to run the entire branch. He decided to go without discussing it with me.

Within a few months, checks stopped coming to pay the bills. He had forgotten entirely about us. Our "perfect family" was falling apart right before my eyes. Each day it was getting worse. I discovered he was having affairs with women he met while on business trips. They took precedence over his family. He became proud and flaunted his affairs. He ignored my calls and was no longer interested in committing to his vows to me.

I snapped, just like the popular TV show, "*Snapped.*" I wanted him dead. I no longer had faith. My failures in marriage had consumed my mental state–this was the breaking point. During a routine visit with my gynecologist, I was in a trance-like state and said, "When my husband gets home from this trip, I will be home waiting to kill him the moment he walks through the door."

The doctor immediately put me in an ambulance, three months pregnant, and sent me to the mental ward of a nearby hospital. I was diagnosed with bipolar disorder related to pregnancy, and severe depression. At the hospital, the doctors did not want to give me medication, only psychotherapy, or, as they often call it, "talk therapy."

I was in the hospital for almost two weeks. I had the urge to give up due to the constant feelings of failure. I didn't deserve to bring another child into this world. I wanted to die. I watched other patients walk around like zombies, one had drunk an entire bottle of Lysol, another had jumped out of a four-story window, and one had been an executive who had worked too hard. After seeing these patients, I thought about my role as a mother. I had a responsibility to heal for the sake of my children.

One day, my father said, "Tonya, you have to get out of there, because we don't have *mental* people in our family."

I encountered the spirit of survival. I had to make it out of the mental ward for *my* family. I made a concerted effort to pray, listen to the therapist, and fully cooperate in group therapy. I even got to make dog leashes for our pets. I accomplished my mission of getting out of there and promised myself I would never return.

We lost our lovely home. I divorced my husband while I was still breastfeeding our baby. I moved the kids to a townhouse that I could afford to rent. My perfect family may have fallen apart, but I was determined to protect my mind and spirit for my children's sake, despite everything else. I vowed to them that I would eventually get it right.

Years later, I rekindled a relationship with an old friend who lived in the Midwest. A year later, we had a beautiful church wedding, costing us thirty-thousand dollars. This marriage lasted three months. Through marital counseling, he told me he was still in love with his ex-wife. I sent him packing immediately after that therapy session. I apologized to my kids again.

I threw myself into work and decided to take college seriously and finish. For years, I had become a career student with no concrete goals in mind. I eventually got my business degree and began studying for my

Master of Business Administration (MBA). I even bought a four-bed-room townhome in a beautiful neighborhood.

Years later, I went on a double date and was introduced to the most intelligent man I had ever met. We hit it off. He asked for my number. Months later, he suggested we date exclusively. I fell in love with him, gravitating to his intelligence. He prepared delicious meals, and he loved my three kids.

I felt God had indeed answered my prayers. He was god-fearing, in-telligent, had a job as an engineer and was about to retire. He had me in tears due to the heart-wrenching stories he shared with me, one of which, his wife had died in a helicopter accident while serving overseas.

After less than twelve months of dating, he asked me to marry him. I said, "Yes." My family and church family liked him a lot. He was ex-tremely outgoing. We went to marriage counseling through my church for six weeks. It occurred to me that I didn't know his parents, although he knew my family. I asked him about it, and he said they were estranged, and he went on with more heart-filled stories. Red flags were flying all around me, but I chose to ignore them. Besides, no one is perfect, cer-tainly not me, so how could I judge?

As I put on my ivory-colored wedding gown, I noticed it was tight in my mid-section. It suddenly occurred to me that I had missed my period. How could this be? Three kids were enough, and besides, I was in my early forties. Also, my fiancée had told me he had a vasectomy.

Days later, my gynecologist confirmed I was pregnant. Then, she said, "No worries. You are too old and will probably miscarry in a few weeks." Her comments hurt me, because if a fetus was inside of me, I wanted it there for nine months.

I told my future husband the news. He was ecstatic! I asked him if he really had a vasectomy, but he strategically changed the subject.

At the chapel, I felt a strong urge to pull away from my son who was giving me away. I wanted to run towards the closest exit. But I didn't. I shrugged at the feeling because I thought this time, it was due to the embarrassment I felt, doing this yet again. But as I glanced around the small chapel, only my family was there. Where was his family? He said they were not coming, and friends got lost. I was apprehensive, but I held his hands, looked him in his eyes, and said, "I do." My new baby will need his father, and my other kids will need him too.

He went back to work as an engineer. I continued my MBA studies while working full time and raising the kids. We celebrated the birth of our baby boy, and the oldest daughter had a baby girl. Yes, two babies, at the same time in the same home! We were making it all work.

We decided to look for a new home since the townhouse was bursting at the seams. We found the perfect home. Just before closing, they said we could not proceed because my husband owed too much child support. Child support? For what child? He neglected to tell me he had a kid that he owed child support. When confronted, he said, "I'm only a Big Brother to the kid; he's not mine." He assured me it was a lie, and he would straighten it out.

Within days, he came home with a letter from the loan company. We were going to close on a big four-bedroom home with lots of acres for our future dream swimming pool! I remember nursing my baby boy when the realtor introduced us to the owner who was there to show us around. I always wanted a home with a big yard and pool for my kids.

The morning of closing, my husband was pacing the floor as if he was suffering from anxiety. He stopped abruptly and said, "God told me not to go to closing."

I became numb. I could have lost it again, another betrayal. But this amazing feeling came over me, I felt God's covering, and for the first time in my life, I asked Him to reveal what else I needed to know. I decided I should no longer make decisions without praying first.

Months later, I discovered my husband's first wife wasn't dead from a helicopter accident; she was alive and well. They had two adult children. The kid he said he was only a Big Brother to *was* his biological child. I married a narcissist. Our entire eight years of marriage were a lie. He is a bigamist who is still legally married to his first wife of over thirty-five years.

At that moment, I realized I already had the perfect family, my four children. I didn't need an uncommitted husband to complete my family. So, I asked the bigamist to leave my home. By that time, my baby boy was eight years old. I no longer felt like a failure and no longer had an urge to marry again.

I decided it was time to embrace the inner child who witnessed what my dad did to my mom when I was only six years old. I went back to therapy, realizing that I was the common denominator in the madness. If I wanted to see changes in my life, I had to be the change. I had to own my role in my pain. I joined a new church family and made my prayer life became a priority again. I began to see that my marriages were not failures because three of those marriages bore me four exceptional children. We were just not evenly yoked. Marriage proposals should be a win-win for all parties for them to be successful, especially with kids involved. As my favorite scripture says, "All things work together for good," Romans 8:28.

My obsession for obtaining the perfect family was the manifestation of a deferred dream to impact lives worldwide! I formed the company, I am Still a Rose, LLC, with a mission to "Light up the world by empowering women to move beyond the pain of their past to a place of new beginnings to include self-worth and wholeness." My past pain has cultivated my business into becoming a tool for helping women. I coach women, have speaking engagements, am a published author, facilitate sell-out inspirational events, and built apparel and product brands for both men and women because I realized men hurt, too. Brokenness begets brokenness.

We need to heal and be whole before getting married. I am an improved version of myself by accepting my past and forgiving myself and others. I am grateful for those that have great marriages and have not dismissed the thought of trying marriage again someday.

Sometimes you must get through it to get to it, your destination. Giving up should never be an option because it is temporary. Reflecting on my past, I would not change anything because I appreciate who I have become. I am now a confident single woman, raising my kids by myself with a village to help. I am not alone. God is always with me.

I am the perfection of God's image who created me. I am a rose and will always be a rose! When I was six years old, witnessing my mother's abuse, I was a rose. As I loved my husbands, each one of them, I was a rose. As I looked for perfection, I was a rose. No matter what stage of life I am in, I will continue to be a rose. I am that beautiful rose that requires fertilizing, self-love, and nurturing. My motto is, "When life brings you thorns, be the rose!" I am now content as a single mother, healed and whole.

TRAPPED IN THAT DARK PLACE

TAMRA T BUSH

WHAT IN THE WORLD? Tay thought to herself while cooking dinner in the kitchen? "What is all that noise upstairs?" she yelled aloud, as a wave of anxiety overcame her. Her eyebrows crinkled, her face frowned up, and her heart started beating fast! Loud, unexpected noises would mentally take her to the place that she didn't want to go, where she was left as a child. That dark place where she stayed trapped, day after day. Tay didn't know how to get out, and no one could help her. It was like climbing an escalator that never stopped or being out of air with no ability to take a deep breath. This was her place of torment, terror, anxiety, and uncertainty for many years. She was a hostage. Why did God choose for her to be in this place? You see, we know that everything is according to HIS will, so really, should there be a question that the things in her life were supposed to happen? Why do we question the bad things but not the good things? Maybe this was a part of human nature.

In a matter of seconds, Tay's mind flashed back to the night she walked to the store with her mom, Gloria. Tay was little, so her mother held her hand during the walk. It was a fast walk, just a few minutes time from the house, up the street, and back. She can't recall exactly what her mom bought from the store; maybe it was some medicine. She just remembered her mother carrying what she had purchased in a brown paper bag.

When Tay and her mom arrived back at the house, her father, Darroll , wasn't home; however, he arrived shortly after they did. Somehow, he knew they had left the house and immediately became furious.

"I told you not to leave this house. Get upstairs!" he yelled multiple times in Gloria's face. "Get up there now!"

As Gloria started to walk slowly up the stairs, Darroll pushed her because she wasn't moving fast enough. When she got to the top of the stairs, he shoved her into the room but didn't close the door all the way.

Tay sat at the top of the steps and watched in horror as Darroll wailed an attack on her mother. She cried and covered her ears, trying to block the sound of the thunderous pounding from each punch as her father pummeled her mother's body. Then she heard the sound of her mother's body hitting the hard, wooden floor. Tay just wanted this beating to be over.

The grunts she heard from the impact of each punch to her mother's body are still vivid in her memory. No matter how hard she has tried to dismiss the thoughts, the memories still gripped her.

Tay was soon yanked back in time, remembering that her father wore black silky socks that night. As he punched her mother repeatedly, his feet would slip on the floor. Her mother balled herself up as tightly as she could and covered her head to ward off the blows, but it didn't matter. He continued to punch her in the body and in the head. Wherever his punches landed, her mother's body seemed to absorb them all; until finally, his fit of rage was over, and he walked away. This was one of the earliest memories Tay had of her father's violent attacks. She was only three or four years old.

Tay snapped out of her thoughts, and her mind brought her back to the current day; she was cooking in the kitchen. She immediately ran upstairs to investigate the ruckus she was hearing. The bumping and jumping led her to a door at the top of the steps. She opened the door to her son's bedroom to find him playing and having fun by himself as children do. She realized that memories of the past had been triggered by the noise her son was making. There was a mix of emotions that came over her.

Butterflies

Tay's memories flooded her mind once again. She was downstairs watching TV when a loud scream echoed through the house. It scared her and shook her to her core. This was a cry of distress and agony. The screaming sent chills through her body so much that she started shaking, and her stomach started hurting. Her body always instantly and uncontrollably reacted to these sounds of violence. What was going on upstairs? What did her dad do to her mother this time?

Tay knew it was nighttime outside because she could see the darkness through the screen door in the kitchen. The back door was almost always left open during the summertime, but the screen door was locked. All the lights were off downstairs, except for the dim light coming from the TV. This was the type of light she would see while she was dreaming. Only this was real life.

Someone was coming down the stairs, but Tay didn't know whose face would appear around the corner. The stairwell was behind a wall, and unless she was sitting at the bottom of the steps, she could never see who was coming until they reached the bottom of the stairway. Her heart began racing. The footsteps were slow, far apart, and unsteady, as if the person coming down the steps was hurt.

Tay sat there, completely paralyzed, as she counted the sound from those wooden steps. There were thirteen steps, from the top of the stairs to the bottom, and each step made a different sound. She remembers that number because, as a child, she had run up and down those stairs hundreds of times. Every time she ran down the steps, she played a little tune in her head that she made up.

Her heart seemed to pause as she saw her mother come around the corner. Her mother's face was red, eyes welled up with tears, and blood dripping from her hand. When she looked closer at her mother, she realized there was blood dripping everywhere! Her mother immediately made her way through the living room into the kitchen, to the phone on the wall by the back door. She remembers her mother picking up the phone and bracing it between her ear and shoulder, but she dropped the phone as she began to hyperventilate because of the excruciating pain in her hand. Gloria was trying to call somebody, anybody, for help!

Tay remembers seeing her mother holding her hand and realizing that she was in so much pain. But as a little girl, Tay didn't know what to do to help her mother. So, she just sat there staring and looking around the room. She can't remember what she said to her mother, if anything at all. However, she does remember getting on the phone and telling the operator what her mom told her to say, "My mom and dad were moving the bed, and the bed fell on her hand. She needs help." She knew deep down inside that wasn't true, but her only thought was doing what her mother asked her to do. She will never know what happened in the room that day, only her mother and father knew the truth.

While all of this was happening, Tay's father came downstairs and stood there, watching her mother struggle. She recalled looking at her father's hands. As a child, she always looked at his hands. His hands were big, rough with calluses, and had knuckles that were thick and bulged out. She was obsessed with his hands because they were the weapons he used against her mother. So much hate, violence, and rage came from those hands.

That night, Tay watched in fear, as her father stood glaring at her mother, while rubbing his right thumb and middle finger together. He had a habit of doing that all the time. Maybe he did this when he was thinking or contemplating something. Tay didn't know why. He just stood there looking at her mother cry. It's as if he was trying to figure out what to do. By his demeanor and body language, Tay knew that he had done this to her mother, and it wasn't an accident! The look in his eyes was not that of remorse or even sympathy. Maybe he knew that he had to do something to keep the police or ambulance from showing up at the house. So, he grabbed Gloria by the shoulders, walked her out the door to the car, and drove off. They left without saying a word.

Tay doesn't recall where her brother was that night or if he was even home. She does, however, remember being a young child left at home during the night because her parents quickly exited the house and closed the door behind them without telling her where they were going or when they would return. She wasn't scared of being left home alone; she was more afraid about her mom having to go to the hospital.

While waiting for her parents to come home, Tay had fallen asleep on the floor downstairs. A few hours later, in the early hours of the morning, her parents came home. When the back door opened, it woke her up. Her mom's hand was wrapped up, and she was still whimpering and moaning from the pain. She made her way upstairs to the bedroom. Tay recalls that it took her mother a while to settle down. Her moaning eventually stopped when she fell asleep.

Her dad never uttered one word to anyone the entire time. But Tay noticed he did not attempt to follow her mother upstairs; instead, he slept on the couch that night.

The First Man She Ever Loved

Darroll was a black man living in America. He was a hardworking man who was handsome and attractive in his youth. As a provider, he made sound, reasonable decisions when it came to money and finances. However, when it came to marriage, family, and love, he exhibited poor judgment and horrible decision-making skills. He smoked a little weed and loved his beer. His fits of rage didn't come as a result of intoxication or substance abuse, they came from somewhere deep within him.

Tay looked up to her father, but as a little girl who loved her father, to witness his level of anger and abuse on a regular basis, was absolutely terrifying. The calm before the storm was the thing that created the most anxiety for Tay growing up. Was today going to be a good day or a bad day? What would set him off to beat her mother up today? Those were the questions in her head every single day, as everyone in her house tip-toed around him. She never knew when the next loud rumble would break out. She would count the days between "violent events" and was thankful anytime she could laugh with her mom and dad and get a peaceful night's sleep.

As a child, Tay hated to leave the house to go outside and play because she knew that when her parents were in the house alone, her father would terrorize her mother even more. She remembers one day she had made her way back to the house after playing with her friends. The front door was open and she could see inside. So, she peeked in and saw her parents standing in the living room. No one seemed to notice Tay. She wasn't sure what her father was doing to her mother, but Tay was scared because her mother looked distressed.

When her mother saw her standing there, she looked at Tay and uttered, "Help me."

Tay was just a little girl and didn't know what to do. So, she just stood there with a blank stare looking in the house until her father walked up to the door and closed it in her face. When Tay was allowed in the house, there was no discussion on what happened to her mother.

If there were more than a few days between fights, her father would find any reason to hit her mother. Tay hated to think of it this way, but it was as if he needed a fix.

The walls were very thin in the projects where they lived, and one time, Tay could hear the next door neighbor beating on his wife. She was frightened by the familiar sounds of someone being beaten. Why did violence seem to surround her?

Her father noticed she was listening to the fighting next door. He looked at her and said, "Guess I'm not the only one," and smiled. There was something wicked about her father. He was a demon inside of a man's body.

There were so many flashes in Tay's mind of the fights her parents had when she was growing up that they became a part of her being. All of it was traumatizing, yet it was the norm in her household, but she NEVER got used to it. There was no calling the ambulance, police, or getting other family members involved. There was no counseling that took place to heal her parents' marriage, help her father confront his fits of rage, or help her mother break free from being an abused wife. She witnessed things that a child should never see or hear at any age. Because of this, she suffered from anxiety, obesity, constant jitters, re-occurring dreams that lasted for years, and issues in her own intimate relationships as an adult. She was a child who saw her mother get pushed down, choked, stabbed, and punched.

You never think about a tragic incident occurring when someone is just doing a simple chore around the house. However, Tay still thinks back to the day that her mom was standing at the kitchen sink washing dishes when her father came up behind her and started digging a knife in her back for no reason. Her mother's face changed as she endured pain from the knife being poked in her back. Gloria didn't utter one sound in that moment. A few seconds later, after he stopped pushing the knife into her body, her mother finished washing the dishes and did other tasks around the house.

Tay hoped her father would get rid of the sharp knives, but he said he kept the big knives around the house for cutting meat. Tay knew he wasn't using the knives just on meat. So, this frightened her, and she always feared the worst would happen.

One night, Darroll and Gloria were up late arguing. Tay was also awake and was looking out of her bedroom door. She remembers seeing her father come out of the bedroom and go downstairs. When he came back, he had a knife in his hand and walked back into the bedroom with it. Tay had a hard time falling asleep, dreading what might be happening to her mother.

The very next day, when Tay didn't see her mother before she went to school that morning, she told her teacher that her father had killed her mother. No one believed her, and nothing ever happened as a result of what she reported to her teacher. The school staff never called child protective services or the police. No one knew what was going on in her house, nor what Tay had to put up with day in and day out.

When Tay got home from school, she slowly opened the front door, afraid of what she might find. She was shocked to see her mother was home and was not hurt. Her mother had gone to work that day and came home as usual.

One day, Tay told her aunt that her father beat up her mother all of the time.

"No, he doesn't, stop lying," her aunt said.

So, Tay started keeping it to herself because the people she told either didn't believe her or they were in denial. Looking back, it's insane how the family swept things like this under the rug. When this is done, all it does is protects the abuser and normalizes their toxic behavior. When Tay was much older, she remembers having a conversation with her father. After living alone for years, her father described a time when he couldn't look at himself in the mirror, so he covered up all the mirrors in his house. He said he was so mad one day that he punched the glass. She remembers him saying that he couldn't stand himself, but he never came out to express the exact reason why he was feeling this way. It seems as if his demons were finally coming back to haunt him.

There were some bad things that happened to Darroll over the years after his divorce from Gloria. He may have repented in private, but he never publicly apologized to Gloria for treating her so badly during their marriage. Even as the mother of his only child, Darroll didn't have enough compassion in his heart for Gloria to treat her like a human being, the woman he married and proclaimed to love.

Why Didn't She Love Herself Enough?

Gloria was a social butterfly. Her bubbly personality, intelligence, hearty laugh, nurturing ways, high cheekbones, thin waist, big hips, and beautiful smile were not enough for the men in her mother's life to do right by her. These things were also not enough for Gloria to see the value in herself. Tragically enough, she stayed in a cycle of abuse. She was also trapped in that dark place. She didn't realize that when she left the first toxic relationship and didn't heal from what attracted her to her first husband, she continued to meet the same abuser again, but in a different person. For a good portion of her life, did Gloria's self-identity reflect the one she loved? When she looked in the mirror, what did she see? Only she knows the answer to that question.

Tay tried to understand what was going on in her mother's mind, causing her to stay and endure all this abuse. She had seen her mother go to the end of the world and back again for the men she loved, which caused Tay to ask herself, *What is it to gain if these men fail to appreciate my mother for who she is?* The lack of value and human decency that some men fail to place on the women who love and support them is completely inconceivable.

However, women must get better at identifying abuse and red flags in the beginning of their relationship and get out early to save their own lives. No matter how much you love a person, violence is not a form of love; it doesn't matter how you look at it. If he hits you once, he will hit you again. We, as human beings, are all birthed from a woman. To abuse the very entity that gave you life, goes against God's will and the flow of nature. It is unimaginable.

Being a child of a mother that was severely abused has had a lifelong effect on Tay emotionally, and psychologically. It isn't just the fact of witnessing so much violence, it is also the fear that some of the traits of her father are present in her. Tay has struggled to control her emotions over the years. As an adult, she is determined to be very intentional in being different from her father, while consistently visualizing herself in a better place, so that she can have the love and peace within her own marriage that she didn't see growing up.

Tay's parents were the first example to her of what a relationship looks like. Therefore, her mind was distorted in regards to what real love looks like, causing her to accept different forms of abuse in her own life. One thing she knows for sure is that it has been a long journey to get to a point of really addressing these issues in her life which were caused by the trauma she experienced as a child. She knows it's trauma and should be acknowledged as such.

Unfortunately, there is still a perpetual cycle of abuse and secrecy in her extended family, on both sides, that must be broken. But Tay now realizes how powerful she is, in being able to bring light to this subject through discussion, and overcome her own obstacles caused by the trauma she hid behind for so long.

No matter how painful it may be, abusers need to be exposed and held accountable for their actions. The only way to break the cycle is to be open to discuss these things as a family so that the healing process can begin. If we fail to do the work, our dreams will indeed be deferred.

FREEDOM FROM THE MASK OF SECRECY

PATTY LAUTERJUNG

When you were a child, did you ever have a nightmare? How did you feel when you woke up? Frightened of the dark? Hysterical? Was someone there to comfort you and help you go back to sleep? I had nightmares as a child and teenager. My mother was always there to turn on the light, put her loving arms around me, and say, "Patricia, I'm here. It was only a dream." Sometimes she sang *Jesus Loves Me*, and I always felt better. But one time, Mother wasn't there to comfort me after the most traumatic nightmare of my life.

In April 2016, I sat on the couch talking to my husband, Paul. "Last weekend was frightful, but I want you to know I forgive you. After thirty years of marriage, we will get through this together." Suddenly, there was a loud banging on the front door. I walked over to peer out the blinds. I recognized the guy from the local TV news. I opened the door just enough to put my head out.

The reporter thrust a microphone in my face. "Can I ask you a few questions?" A cameraman stood at the end of the walkway. Sadly, I knew why the reporter was there. I shook my head no, stepped back, closed the door, and locked it. I frantically ran around to close all the blinds. I fought back tears and thought, *What the hell just happened? How did I get here?*

When you were young, what dreams did you have about your future? Mine were like most girls my age--marry Prince Charming, have a baby, own a dream home, and live *happily ever after*. I never forgot about my dream through high school and college—to find my prince-- but I had to kiss a lot of frogs along the way!

I had a great job after college, went to church, joined the choir, volunteered for youth ministry, but I still longed for Prince Charming. During a women's retreat in May 1985, I wrote in my Bible at the end of Proverbs 31--the ideal wife chapter--the qualities I wanted in a husband. I wanted God to know who I was looking for.

About a year later, I sat in church mesmerized by the tenor voice of the soloist. I thought, *Who is that handsome guy with the magnificent voice?* When he left with another woman, I sighed and forgot about him.

Two weeks later at church, the handsome guy stood near my car. I said hello, and we talked for a while. Paul invited me to lunch, and we started dating. He was fun, brought flowers, and sang love songs to me. I believed God had answered my prayer.

October 1987, I walked down the aisle in a beautiful white wedding dress. That night, Paul signed his name, the date, and wrote "That's me!" at the bottom of my Proverbs 31 list. My childhood dream was coming true.

One morning in September 1988, we sat at the kitchen table and Paul said, "Where is my blue shirt? I want to wear it to work."

"I washed it last night and need to iron it."

"Go iron it now," he said sternly.

"I have to leave for work. I'll iron it when I get home. There is an ironed white shirt in the closet."

Paul stood up, glared down at me and said, "I want my blue one! You need to be submissive to me!"

I stared at him confused and said, "Yes, but not right now."

Without warning, Paul punched the side of my face with his fist, knocking my glasses to the floor. For a few seconds I couldn't see, throbbing pain radiated near my eye. With trembling hands, I wiped away the tears. "Why did you hit me?"

"I'm sorry. I didn't mean to," he said and knelt down to hug me.

"Get away from me!" I yelled and ran into the bathroom. "Oh, my God! My face is bleeding and my eye is swelling!"

Later, Paul came downstairs wearing his white shirt. "I'm sorry. Please forgive me. That will never happen again." I glared at him but didn't say a word. He frowned and walked out the front door.

As I glanced at my reflection in the mirror, I felt ashamed. I called my mother. She comforted my pain with words of love. We decided not to tell Dad because of what he might do to Paul. I stayed home from work until my eye healed.

A year later, I was so excited to find out I was pregnant. I was almost forty and ready to quit work to stay home as a full-time mother. Our baby was due in March.

One afternoon, I got angry with Paul. "I'm tired of you sitting in front of the TV and not helping me clean the house."

He glared at me, stood up, and shoved me hard onto the floor. I screamed, "Oh dear God. My baby! My baby!"

"You're fine. Stop being hysterical," he said. I held back the tears. I didn't tell anyone, not even my doctor. Thankfully, Paul Jr. was born a healthy, happy baby.

Two years later, we moved to a larger home, but without my income we used credit cards to pay our bills. We argued about money and blamed each other for the rapidly increasing debt. The cycle of Paul's violent anger, followed by empty apologies, started again with him hitting and shoving me. I believed him that my critical remarks caused his loss of control. I felt insecure and focused my attention on nurturing Paul Jr. We attended church...but nobody knew our secret.

In college, I had excellent grades in English; so I started a proofreading business to add to our income. However, it wasn't enough because over the next seven years our finances were a disaster. Our marriage suffered from ongoing conflict. We went to counseling, marriage seminars, read books, signed agreements, and were accountable to others.

Typically, any behavior change is temporary. Permanent change takes commitment, discipline, and a lot of work. The reality is, we can only change ourselves. People don't change unless they choose to.

In April 2003, I screamed with excitement when we moved to our beautiful dream home in Roseville, CA. We attended Bayside Church, a thriving fellowship with opportunities for spiritual growth and a fabulous youth group for our teenage son. For the next thirteen years, my relationship with God and involvement at church kept my life and marriage together.

There's a term called *trauma bonding*. It is a deep, emotional attachment created by a cycle of abuse, kindness, and intimacy. The *abusive* person has qualities that include being charming but emotionally unpredictable, thoughtful, and gives gifts and physical affection. They blame you for their behavior, apologize for the abuse, and don't keep promises to change. The abuser tries to isolate you from others and even says you are their soulmate and meant to be together.

The *abused* person has traits that include continued trust and belief the abuser will change, with more focus on special times together. They feel embarrassed and shameful for their situation, protect the abuser and relationship through secrets, and feel unable to leave for reasons like finances, children, and fear of safety.

The Bible says in Matthew 18:21-22, "Then Peter asked Jesus, 'Lord, how many times shall I forgive my brother or sister who sins against me? Up to seven times?'" Jesus answered, "I tell you, not seven times, but seventy-seven times." The Christian principle of *forgiveness* is to forgive others when they sin against us, just as God has forgiven us for our sins.

Scripture is not a weapon for sinful, harmful behavior or to justify forgiveness. Paul combined forgiveness with the action to *forget* and said, "The Bible commands you to forgive." *Forgive and forget* was used to manipulate me to believe his behavior would change if I always forgave him and stopped bringing up the past.

If you looked at my life based on photos, you might think, *Patty has such a fun and interesting life. She always looks happy.* I have enjoyed a lot of interesting experiences and fun times, including during my marriage. I often choose to make the best of a situation and live by Mother's words, "Patricia, you can do anything you put your mind to. Life is too short to worry all the time. Be happy and enjoy it."

I decided to change the unhealthy direction of my life and joined a program at Bayside called Celebrate Recovery. It is a Christ-centered, twelve-step recovery program that provides support to people who struggle with any type of addiction, hurt, or habit. It is a safe place to work through issues that affect your life. With weekly teaching, worship, fellowship, and small group support, I learned how to take responsibility for my actions instead of blaming others, let go of control, ask forgiveness for my behavior, and for the first time...share my secrets. I found freedom from my people-pleasing habits and made self-care a priority.

The healthy behavior I learned gave me confidence and strength to set boundaries and stand up for myself. The turning point came one afternoon when Paul came towards me with his clenched fist, ready to hit me. I stood up tall, raised my hand in the air, looked him straight in the eye and said, "If you hit me, I will call the police."

He scowled, "You wouldn't dare call the police. You would be too embarrassed."

"No, you would be embarrassed when your name is in the newspaper tomorrow under police reports." He called me an abusive name, left the room, and never hit me again. Change happened when I knew exactly what I wanted, clearly communicated it, and stood my ground.

Paul Jr. was now in his twenties, attended a local college, played guitar on the church worship team, and dated Kelly, who he met on a church mission trip. He and Kelly married in November 2013. I worried that our marriage problems negatively affected him. What I found was Paul Jr. was a good husband, cherished Kelly, they enjoyed each other, were financially responsible, and both had a solid relationship with God. I prayed for what I wanted next—grandchildren!

In February 2014, my ninety-eight-year-old mother suddenly got ill from a leg infection. Her sharp mind quickly declined, she needed frequent care, and moved into our home. Sometimes at night, I heard her cry out. I ran to her room, turned on the light, gently stroked her hair, and sang *Jesus Loves Me* until she fell asleep. On March 3rd, Mother peacefully passed into the arms of Jesus. I miss her beyond words. Thankfully, she never witnessed her child's most traumatic nightmare.

One Sunday after church, my husband, Paul, said, "Remember a detective came by three weeks ago when I was at work?"

"Yes, he told me there was an incident at the gym and for you to call him."

"Well, I talked to him twice," Paul said.

"Why didn't you tell me sooner?"

"I was afraid you would divorce me. I need to confess, but you must promise not to tell anyone," he said with tears in his eyes. Paul began to reveal his dark secret. When he was done, he begged for forgiveness.

I had mixed emotions, but I tearfully said, "I forgive you. We will get through this together."

For the next two weeks, I endured intense, emotional turmoil. My promise to Paul not to tell anyone was a horrible mistake. I put on a cheerful mask of secrecy, but headaches and nausea plagued my body. The deception around everyone, including not telling my son, sacrificed my emotional freedom as I protected the man I once believed was Prince Charming.

I prayed for direction on what to do, but God seemed to be silent. I thought, *The Bible says God works all things together for His good. I need to wait and trust Him.* I felt imprisoned with my silence and asked Paul to tell Paul Jr.

One morning, I turned on the news and was devastated to see Paul's photo and hear the reporter say, "This man was arrested Friday on suspicion of molesting someone. Police believe there may be other victims out there." I was stunned when he said, "We tried to interview an unidentified woman who wouldn't speak to us." I looked in horror as I saw myself on TV peering out our front door.

I went into complete isolation. My dream home became a prison. I kept the shades pulled and only went out late at night for groceries. Phone calls, text messages, and private Facebook comments overwhelmed me.

Some friends and family didn't know what to say and were silent, while others wouldn't acknowledge me when I said hello. At first, their reactions felt hurtful. I was encouraged when some friends said, "It's not your fault. Are you okay? How is Paul Jr.? What can I do to help you? Can I take you to coffee or lunch?" The most surprising response was, "Let me tell you about the time my name was in the news."

Paul's legal case lasted a year. The uncertainty of a court decision and sentence pulled me closer to God. I fell on my knees in prayer, tears streaming down my face, asking, *How did I get to this awful place in my life?* I longed to know God's purpose for me in all this chaos.

God had waited for me to take off the mask of secrecy to reveal my true self and move me toward His purpose. I decided to expose my years of lies, sinful behavior, and secrets to my counselor and a few close friends. I discovered an inner strength and a new perspective on who I was and the life I wanted. The change He wanted to make would manifest itself through His plan.

Paul was convicted of a misdemeanor charge of indecent exposure. The sentence included three months in jail, three years on probation, and a lifetime registration as a sex offender.

My time alone for three months was an unfamiliar experience. The peace and freedom from daily tension and conflict was a significant blessing. There were fewer tears and more smiles on my face and joy in my heart. I listened to Christian music and danced and sang around the house. I laughed with friends and enjoyed relaxing walks. Now, I understand why I don't deserve to be abused by anyone, yet I continued to hope for a better marriage.

When Paul came home from jail, my peace and freedom left. I felt imprisoned again when conflict and emotional and verbal abuse quickly returned. He called me insulting names, minimized my feelings, mocked what I said, and shamed me for trying to change. The mental abuse made me question my sanity, perception of reality, and memory.

Every month, the police pounded on our door, walked through the house, and interrogated us. My heart raced, I held back tears, and felt punished and violated for something that wasn't my fault. I questioned God about my future. "Lord, my dream has become a nightmare! Do You want me to share Paul's consequences for the rest of my life? I'm exhausted and confused, and don't know if You want me to stay or leave." I trusted God would answer, but I had to wait on Him.

God provided me with a new dream. Paul Jr. and Kelly invited me to lunch and gave me a toy guitar with a sign that read, "Future rock star joining the band in 2018." I jumped up and down with excitement, and tears of joy filled my eyes!

Despite years of counseling and Paul promising to do better, the emotional and verbal assaults continued. I no longer wanted to hold onto false hope that my marriage would get better. This led to a life-changing decision.

A few weeks later, Paul and I met with two pastors from church. We discussed the *Terms of Separation* that he and I agreed to. Paul used the separation time to be with family and friends in southern California because his mother had just passed away.

I was alone again, and my carefree dancing and positive spirit returned. People had the same response. "You are a different person without Paul. God doesn't expect you to stay in an abusive relationship. Do you want to live that way the rest of your life?"

"No, I don't want to be abused ever again, but I don't believe God has released me from the marriage yet." I thought about what they said and prayed every day that God would show me what to do.

One morning, as I read my Bible and prayed, God spoke to me through my thoughts. He said, "I have plans for you that are greater than your life now. You have faithfully waited on Me. I release you from your marriage." My body relaxed, and I took a few deep breaths. I closed my eyes as I thanked God for His answer and thought about the blessing of a better life.

With God's green light of release, adamant I would not live with any abuse, and fed up with someone who pulled me down when I sought God's best, I boldly moved forward with a divorce. I got advice from my counselor, talked to a few people I respected and trusted, and wrote the steps I needed to take. I hired an excellent attorney, Carsen Tazi, and felt confident in her and the journey ahead. I changed the locks on the doors, got security cameras, and felt safe.

I called Paul and told him about the divorce. He was angry and started to criticize me.

I said, "Goodbye, Paul," and hung up the phone. I felt good about my decision and how I handled myself. Paul never entered our home again until we met with the realtor. The house sold quickly. I was content to live in my peaceful apartment.

In early 2019, Paul Jr. came to me and said, "Kelly and I are thinking about moving to North Carolina." I immediately said, "I'm going with you!" My beautiful granddaughter Addison was a year old, and I didn't want distance to separate us. The embrace of her tiny body next to mine brought countless smiles to my face and kisses to hers. Now, my life as a grandmother overflows with exciting new experiences, heightened energy, and the delightful sound of laughter.

By August 2019, we had moved to Charlotte, NC. I loved the area and friendly people, quickly made friends, and immediately got involved at Elevation Church. God brought me to a beautiful, yet unfamiliar part of the country to show me the greater plans He had promised.

My divorce was plagued by money disagreements, which caused the divorce settlement to drag on for two years. Again, God spoke to me, "The stress and time over money imprisons you. Let it go and move on. Trust Me." So, in March 2020, I settled the divorce. Finally, I savored the sweet taste of freedom. A week later, the world began to shut down due to Covid-19. I marveled at God's timing and was grateful I listened to Him. The long-term investment of trusting God's wisdom I found in the words of Jeremiah 29:11. "For I know the plans I have for you," declares the Lord, "plans to prosper you and not to harm you, plans to give you hope and a future."

The year 2020 was the cornerstone of God's greater journey for me. In July, I joined an award-winning publishing company as an editor, and now my business reaches people worldwide. God continues to reveal more of who He created me to be and provide meaningful opportunities to grow. His promise of a better life for me included healthy and loving family relationships. In September, joy radiated from my heart at the birth of my second granddaughter, Isabella. God's blessing is I leave a legacy for my granddaughters with a story that has a happy ending.

Now, when I glance in the mirror, I see a woman of strength who can share her story of a childhood dream that manifested into God's divine plan for her life. I am free from the mask of secrecy that imprisoned me for many years.

Abuse is colorblind to race, age, and gender. If you recognize any of the harmful behaviors that I experienced, either in your relationships or with someone you know, please get help. Be open to God's power and wisdom to help you change yourself and see what happens to the relationships in your life. Some will end, but those that remain grow stronger. My prayer is that you know you are loved and valued by God. He has great plans for you.

A HEART OF LOVE

AMY HAYES

Have you ever felt like your mind is a rollercoaster of different emotions? Well, congratulations! You're just like me. You have a mind so grey that the only thing that lives there is the constant fear of disappointment. I have learned that disappointments are bound to happen; it goes around like a clock. But if we put our trust in the Lord, it will get better. As Rose Kennedy stated, "It has been said, 'time heals all wounds.' I do not agree. The wounds remain. In time, the mind, protecting its sanity, covers them with scar tissue and the pain lessens. But it is never gone."

At six, I was already used to the sound of my mom crying. Dad would turn her into a punching bag, day and night. The wailing noise pierced my ears as she cried out, begging him to stop. There was nothing my sister and I could do except listen and watch. Begging did not make him stop. Each morning he would wake up and act like nothing was wrong. He walked around as if he was our god.

Mom seemed to carry the pain in her eyes and bruises on her body. "How do you beat your wife and then, ask for sex?" she would lament but still end up in his arms again. And for some reason, I never stopped loving my dad. The pain and the scare that both my sister and I endured was indescribable. I can't ever remember experiencing peace in our home as a little girl. "Just chaos!"

Anytime Dad came home from work, he always fought with my mom. For whatever reason, he seemed to enjoy arguing and fighting with Mom. As a little girl, seeing this traumatized me. We would always walk on eggshells in the house. Mom was not happy, and my sister and I were very fragile emotionally. I can only imagine what my sister felt, being that she was the oldest. There are some things I can remember and some things I don't. My sister and I are four years apart, and I know she experienced far more than I did.

Dad was very mean to us while we were growing up. His drinking had gotten the best of him. We never had the father-daughter bond. I was never daddy's girl, nor was my sister. He never gave us compliments. Can you believe he never called us beautiful? We just swept everything under the rug because even if we had spoken up, we felt there was no one to help us.

I was wrong. I wished I had asked for help. I wish I knew better. I let my fear get in the way. The Bible says, "Be strong and courageous. Do not fear or be in dread of them, for it is the Lord your God who goes with you. He will not leave you or forsake you" (Deuteronomy 31:6).

You, reading this book, never be afraid to ask for help. Don't be ashamed of what people say. Please, learn from my mistakes.

When my Mom gave birth to my brother, I was very jealous since all the attention had shifted from me. My now deceased Auntie would always say, "Amy ain't the baby no more." She said it so much she sounded like a broken record. No child should have to go through this.

One day when my mom asked me to make a bottle for my little brother, I decided to mix his milk with salt out of the bitterness of my little heart. When my mom realized what I had done, she disciplined me–the hard way. I felt really bad and was convicted of my

141

wrongdoing. I didn't understand what I was doing at the time. All I wanted was to be the baby again.

Since that incident, I rebuked the devil whenever he came! I was simply a rebellious little girl who wanted attention.

"Lord, Thank You for forgiveness."

Luke 23:34 says, "Jesus said, 'Father forgive them, for they know not what they are doing.'"

In school, kids could be so cruel and very judgmental at times. I was mocked for my gap tooth and my dark skin. The kids bullied me and called me ugly. It was difficult not being accepted in school, and then, to go home and not be fully accepted by my dad. *Still, I had a heart of love.*

After all these years, I still can't get over all that has happened in my life. Sometimes my sister and I talk about our childhood on the phone. She shares things that happened that I can't remember or maybe I was too young to understand. We went through school wearing shoes and clothes that were too small and not cute. It wasn't easy to go through all that at the time, but I'm glad we have each other to lean on now.

Our Mom did the best she could with what little she had. The glue that held us together was Love. That's what my mom instilled in us. "When the going gets tough, and the tough gets going, love one another." Even today, I can hear my mom's voice saying, "Well, you got to love 'em anyways."

Despite my dad's problems, he had a good job, though. Every year he would take us to Six Flags with our cousins. We had so much fun. But no matter how much happiness we experienced, we still remained sad. No one knew it, though, because we always appeared happy on the outside, but we were so sad on the inside. We wore smiles to keep from crying, because we were forced to face the brutal reality that our dad loved cars more than he loved us. He loved women more than he loved us. The bad certainly outweighed the good.

My sister and I were young. I wish we had enjoyed our childhood like other children. The Bible tells us in Ecclesiastes 11:9, "You who are young, be happy while you are young, and let your heart give you joy in the days of your youth." Sometimes when I think about the things I have gone through, I feel regret. I sometimes think that maybe I should have put salt in my dad's drink. Damn, why didn't I do that?

After all the fighting and numerous cheating incidents, my Mom apparently had enough. She was planning to leave my Dad. She was lying on the couch talking on the phone, telling someone she was going to leave Dad. She said, "This is the final straw. I've had enough!" We weren't sure what she was talking about, but we knew she was serious.

Dad stayed out all night. The next morning, he came home drunk. Before long, they began to argue and fight. We tried our best to ignore it, but our apartment was so small you could hear everything. All of a sudden, we heard screaming. We ran from the bedroom into the front room to find my dad fighting with Mom. Mom ran through the kitchen, trying to exit the back door, but he caught up with her. The demons had a hold of my dad. He quickly grabbed the biggest knife in the kitchen and started stabbing my mom. Blood was everywhere!

Mom was not able to fight him off. She was lying limp on the floor and was covered with blood. She looked like she was near death! She had stab wounds throughout her whole body. After a few minutes, her eyes rolled back in her head, and tears trickled down her face.

My sister and I were terrified! Without thinking, she ran over to our dad and tried to stop him from stabbing our mother.

Dad turned to her with cold, cruel eyes, and said, "Move, before you be next!" And he continued stabbing our mother.

Our father was out of control. How could he do this to his wife, someone he said he loved? And how could he look his own daughter in the face and utter those horrible words?

We knew we had to get help for Mom. So, we ran to the phone and tried calling 911, but dad snatched the phone cord out of the wall and glared at us.

We dashed out the door to the neighbor's house screaming, "Call 911! Our dad is hurting our mom." Soon, we heard the loud sirens, and then the paramedics arrived, along with the police. The policeman arrested my dad. As they led him to the police car, Dad looked at us and smiled. He almost seemed joyful, without a hint of remorse or sorrow, as he said the most horrific thing anyone could ever say to a child, "I done kill your Ma!"

I suddenly felt dizzy and couldn't breathe. *No! that can't be true, I thought!* I was trying to get to my mom as I screamed, "No! No, please don't die, Mamma!"

Then, I heard a paramedic say, "We've got a pulse!

Hearing the sirens and all the commotion, people soon surrounded our apartment. It was like a mob. The streets were filled with bystanders. Everyone on our street was angry and disgusted by what my dad had done.

Soon, grandmama and granddaddy arrived. When she found out what happened to my mother, grandmama cried out, "My baby, Lord, don't let her die!" She kept praying and crying.

My granddaddy had his shotgun with him. He was ready to kill our dad, but grandmama pleaded with him not to kill Daddy. She didn't want to lose her daughter and her husband.

Romans 8:28 says, "God promises to make something good out of the storms that bring devastation to your life."

Now, when I think about that tragic night, I get very emotional. That incident is part of the reason why I couldn't release my book sooner, because the pain is still so deep–it still hurts! Sitting here writing is difficult for me, but I'm determined to get over this hurdle. I know God will give me the strength to finish this story and tell my testimony, because my story might help someone, and it will set me free.

It may be hard to believe, but guess what? Our Mom survived! Shocking, isn't it? She survived over thirty-two stab wounds to her face, chest, under her breast, and all over her arms.

As a result of her wounds, the doctors told Mom that she would have congestive heart failure. But glory to God, my mom has not suffered any major side effects from the wounds.

One day when I was talking to my Mom, she said, "If I had not lain still on the floor, pretending to be dead, your dad would have never stopped stabbing me."

I can't imagine what she was thinking or feeling as she lay on the floor that day. But to me, she was courageous and was a fighter. She fought to live. *She is truly a living testimony—a walking miracle.*

While Mom went through her healing process, we had to live with our grandparents. During this time, we were not allowed to see our dad, nor was he able to come near us. We were thankful being apart from him because it's the most peace we had experienced in a very long time.

Over time, we came to understand that our dad had a lot of secrets he was trying to keep hidden from my mom and us. His life was built around drinking, lying, cheating, and beating on my mom. When he became outraged and lashed out at us, I believe it was out of fear of being exposed. When I reflect back to that awful day, Daddy seemed to be overtaken by demons–like a possessed person, a person with mental problems. It's still hard to believe that he never served criminal time behind bars for what he did to my mother.

Years went by, and Dad continued to drink and drive. One day, he was pulled over and was arrested for driving under the influence. He eventually went to prison, and that's how he paid for his crimes. "Karma is something."

After my mom was healed, we went back to live in the projects. She was trying to move on with her life. Years had gone by, and she was ready to share her life with someone special now that my Dad was no longer in our lives. She started talking to this new dude. Initially, he was nice. Then, one night he came into me and my sister's bedroom. He touched us inappropriately. We didn't know what to say or do to make him stop.

Early the next morning, we told our mom what happened. She looked surprised but didn't say much. We thought she believed us and would break up with him until Mister walked back into our house one day and our mother seemed glad to see him. We were disgusted and afraid.

At night, we locked our bedroom door, but it didn't help because Mister would use a butter knife to pop the lock and come in. We started pushing our dresser in front of the door, thinking that would keep him out. But no, that didn't help. Mister was just like a mouse or rat; he found his way in.

The next day, we told our mom what happened, hoping this time she would believe us. But he denied it. I will never forget how she looked at us in shame. Seeing that nobody was going to listen, we planned for his next visit to our room.

That night, when he came to our room again, we pretended to be asleep. When he tried to touch me inappropriately, I struck his ass on his back as hard as I could. Then, I screamed as loud as I could, "Get outta here!" He ran out of the room, hopping like a kangaroo.

The next morning, we told Mom again, but she still didn't seem to believe us.

"Are y'all thinking the same thing I'm thinking?" My sister and I felt worried that our mom didn't want to hear us out. Perhaps, she was scared that people would find out about him. Or maybe she just feared being alone. It was painful to watch.

Parents, please listen to your children. And children, speak up. If someone is talking to you inappropriately or touching you in your private areas, don't hesitate to tell someone. My sister and I weren't "fast girls," yet this pedophile came at us! He was a very sick-minded man. It was so uncomfortable to be around this evil person.

No one seemed to care about our feelings. We were two little girls who were wounded by our father. Then, we were put into a situation where we were sexually assaulted by a man—our mother's boyfriend. Why were we expected to forgive and forget after others hurt us? Pain, devastation, disappointment, shame, and hurt began overtaking my every thought.

We moved to another city when I was twelve. It was still in the projects, but this time we lived in a townhouse. We were grateful and excited about the move. We enrolled in a new school. We were leaving everything behind except my bed-wetting, which was a result of my anxiety, pain, and fear. But with time, it ceased. As they say, "Time heals all wounds." Thank you, Jesus!

During the summer, one of my friends came to stay with us. One day she came to me with tears in her eyes and said, "Your momma's boyfriend touched my breast!"

I didn't know what to say. I was ashamed and angry. "I'm so sorry. He did the same thing to my sister and me." I couldn't believe he was doing this to other girls.

The next morning, the three of us went to tell my mom. This time she reacted differently. "He's gotta go. I'm fed up with him," she said. So, she put him out.

Mister was not fine. As a matter of a fact, he looked like our dog. So why was mom keeping him around? Maybe for financial support. But how many other girls had he hurt?

Today, as I write my story, I can say with relief, "Mister has now passed away." I hope and pray he repented of his ways and actions.

Parents, please take good care of your children and I continue to say, listen to them.

After everything we had experienced in our childhood, my mom tells us she has forgiven our dad. After all he did to her and to us? It didn't make sense. After he stabbed her, I wanted her to hate him! But James 5:16 reminded me that vengeance is not mine.

The Bible tells us in Matthew 6:14-15, "For if ye forgive men their trespasses, your heavenly Father will also forgive you. But if you do not forgive men their sins, your Father will not forgive your sins."

Reading and studying the Word of God was and still is the best healing for my soul. It assures me that I have *"a heart of love."*

It was shocking that my mom never let bad things affect her good heart. Like Luke 6:28 says, "Bless those who mistreat you." If someone hurt us, she'd pray for them. For years I felt a rollercoaster of emotions but cited this prayer to battle it:

Lord Jesus,

Deliver me from anger. Set me free from bitterness. I thank you for being by my side. Your love never fails me. Your road is the right road. Help me to continue to positively work through each situation and each emotion. In Jesus' name, Amen.

There were times when I told myself I was not going to overcome obstacles, but I did. I have cried a lot over my journey through life, but I'm still standing. It reminds me of a song by Mary J. Blige, "The Living Proof," where she sings about a tough situation that almost took her out, but she survived because the worst was over, and her best days were ahead.

So, believe in yourself! Your past trauma does not define you. Most of all, have faith in God, and He will see you through.

Trying to Build a Relationship with My Dad

Trying to build a relationship with my dad did not happen immediately, considering all the pain he put us through. I have realized that he has gone through his own trauma in the past. We don't talk often, but we bond as much as we can. While going through my own illness, my dad stood by my side.

He has never apologized to us about the pain he caused us. Although, I must say, it would be really nice to hear those words coming from him. If Dad never, ever says I'm sorry, I can finally say that I'm free from the pain, rejection, and resentment. I have made peace with it.

Understand, an apology is not for the other person—it is for you. When you have *A Heart of Love,* you can conquer the world. "Trust the Lord with all your heart, and lean not on your own understanding; In all your ways acknowledge Him, And He shall direct your paths." (Proverbs 3:5-6).

From Pain to Business

In 2017, I started my non-profit organization called, Ames Heart of Love, where we get to pray, help the elderly, and feed the homeless. It was finally something I found joy doing. God has shown me the way. Running a business is not easy, but with God, He shall make a way. He does not give us situations we cannot handle. I was put in a situation for over ten years that caused me not to be able to put time into my business. But I never stopped dreaming and writing down my ideas. I tried to surround myself with positive people that also had *A Heart of Love.* Sometimes, I fell short, but each time I looked at myself in the mirror, I knew I had to get back up and try again. It's not easy trying to suppress your feelings when you have seen and been through so much as a child and teenager. But here I am putting everything I have into what I love, "Ames Heart of Love Ministry."

Ames Heart of Love is doing mighty and great things. I never would have made it without the Lord. Love makes everything feel great. If Ames Heart of Love would not have been birthed, then *A Heart of Love* would have never been written.

To God be the glory.

AFFIRMATIONS

I am enough

Love starts within, and I love me

I am beautiful inside and out

I am a fighter and will never give up

I forgive myself for not believing in me in the past

Write your personal affirmation/s here:

SECTION 4

BLOSSOMING BRAVERY

Certain gifts materialize due to friction, pressure, or pain. Wine is the result of stomping of the grapes; oil is expelled from the crushing of the olives; smooth wood surfaces after it has been chopped, sawed, and sandpapered. Amid adversities, it is hard to find the light. But then bravery kicks in, and when it is all said and done, the results are beautifully refined.

"This is my command—be strong and courageous! Do not be afraid or discouraged. For the Lord your God is with you wherever you go." Joshua 1:9 New Living Translation

GROUNDED IN GRACE - A MOTHER'S JOURNEY THROUGH LOVE AND LOSS

PERMETHA RUDY MILTON

Have you ever been numb, shocked, and felt like you were in a dream? I was a proud, happy-go-lucky mother. I thought I was living the dream, and I felt like I had it all. I was working for a Fortune 500 company, making great money with benefits, and had my own home. Most importantly, I was a mother to my beloved son, Dominique. When I was eighteen years old, I had my one and only child. I was so blessed to graduate high school. Life was great, and we were happy!

I never thought I would have to do it alone. I was co-parenting, and it was working. Raising kids these days is not easy. You need both parents, grandparents, aunts, uncles, and church family. Did I say raising kids these days was easy? Oh, and you need the community too. It took a village to raise my son, Dominique. The foundation was established early on. He went to a Christian in-home, loving, and nurturing day care environment. He then started his journey to Mary's Christian Day School. He was getting everything at home and then some at school. He couldn't escape it. There he learned structure, bible scriptures, learning to share, singing, and at a tender age, he started his journey to becoming a Christian.

Dominique was a musician. He was a charismatic drummer, filled with energy, laughter, and love. He learned at the tender age of six. Genetically he was blessed with talent. His dad and auntie are musicians as well. Dominique was passionate and loved playing the drums. He mastered it and played where he could. We lived in a condo. Can you imagine hearing drums playing next door? Our neighbors got used to it, and so did I. He worked hard to perfect his craft for music and playing. Not to mention he would play on my kitchen table, in the car, and on my coffee table. I said, "Domi," as I affectionately called him, "don't you have drums in your room? Please go in there and play and not on my furniture, son." He would continue to beat as he moved away from the furniture. "Drumz is My Life" is inscribed on his drumsticks. He would take them everywhere because he never knew when the opportunity would arise to play. He didn't want to miss a chance. He was hungry for opportunity and exposure.

On Sundays, Dominique would play in three church services. How did he get to three different services, you ask? You would've thought he was driving. Remember, I told you it takes a village. He would get a ride from his church and then go to my mom's church, which is about fifteen minutes away. His grandmother's church was about forty-five minutes to an hour away, depending on traffic. If he knew a drummer was going to be unavailable to play at church, he would show up. He was determined. Sometimes it took us meeting each other to get Dominique where he had to be to play. He was so loved. We did it!

Dom loved to play football and basketball. He enjoyed both sports, but football was his go-to sport. He was a team player and had great sportsmanship. His first love was playing the drums and music. We enrolled him in a music camp so he could learn how to read music and play with other talented musicians. He enjoyed it!

We did camp for two years. He was a traveler. He then started to travel with our church to conventions around the state of South Carolina. He met a lot of wonderful people. Yes, a lot of young ladies too. He was a charmer and very handsome. He was widely admired. He was so dang special. Did I forget to tell you he was the only grandson on his maternal side and at the time the only grandson on the fraternal side growing up. He later became the oldest grandson of three on his fraternal side. He was cared for, loved, and reared by so many.

I love Dominique more than life. He was my everything. We enjoyed shopping, traveling, dancing, watching movies cuddled up with our own monogrammed throws. We laughed, cried, disagreed, played together, enjoyed go-karts, and going out to eat. He would get so upset when we watched a movie, because I would always fall asleep on him. He vowed to never watch another movie with me again. Let's not talk about my singing. I cannot sing, not a secret. He would say, "Ma, please stop. Just hum. You're hurting my ears." I would laugh so hard. We would normally turn up the music and start getting our praise on as we got dressed for Sunday morning worship at home. Our neighbors loved us! We continued the same energy on the car ride to church. His famous words, "I'm going to make them shout today." We prayed, served, and worshiped together. Both of us were baptized by our Pastor. He knew us, and we had a wonderful relationship with him. It continues today as well.

Dominique continued to serve God and knew Him for himself. Praying at dinner was natural as he became a teenager, and he prayed before going to bed. Oh, how I miss kneeling and praying beside him. The first scripture we learned together was the Twenty-Third Psalm. We started piece by piece until we memorized it. I encourage you to go to Bible study to learn scriptures. I still do. That scripture just spoke to Dominique and me, and we grew from there. Our relationship with God was central in our home. When he went to his grandparents, he would call them both "Ma" as well. Our granny, he would call Granny. They adored him. His favorite dish was macaroni. He loved it. He would come home with leftovers, when one of my one friends would make it. He would ride his bike in the sunshine or rain to get some. He had an appetite. When he went to high school, I gave him his first debit card. His transaction list was routine, McDonald's, Cookout, and Zaxby's.

He was good-looking, slim, and trim. His "drip," as the young people would say, was on point. He never left the house not presentable and always smelled amazing! I taught him at a very young age how to take care of himself, iron his clothes, and look presentable. We had barbers from Charleston, Hilton Head/Bluffton, to Savannah, GA. His haircuts were a pet peeve of mine. I could tell when he went somewhere else. I would wait patiently for him numerous times to get his haircut. I enjoyed being a mother!

On July 19, 2015, at 8:02 p.m., my life changed forever. We had just moved into a new home, and I was still putting things away. I went to work and did not go to church that particular Sunday. I called Dominique to see if he had gone with my mom to church, but he did not. I said, "Okay, Domi, is granny cooking?"

"Yes!" he said.

"I'll see you after work for dinner," I said and proceeded to work. How could I have known that my life would soon be forever changed. Later that day when I arrived home, I was in my room putting away some things. The phone rang. It was Dominique's mentor.

"Have you spoken to Dominique today?"

"Yes, he's at the beach with some friends."

"I got a phone call that Dominique has been shot," he said.

I didn't clearly hear what he said. "WHAT? WHERE?" I asked. "Not my child! He's at the beach. I'm waiting on his dad now. We're going to dinner. I'll call you back." I hung up the phone, screamed hysterically, panicking, and crying. I nervously dialed his dad's number. When he answered, I screamed into the phone, "I just got a call that Dominique has been shot! Where are you?"

"What? I'll be right there," he said.

I hurried and changed clothes, and began pacing the floor, and glancing out the window, waiting impatiently for his dad to arrive. The car finally pulled into the driveway. I dashed out the door and jumped into the car. We prayed and asked God to save our son. We prayed the entire car ride! We are talking about a thirty-minute car ride. We arrived at the well-known beach area which attracts thousands of tourists annually.

The unexpected happened. "My Pumpkin," I screamed as I ran towards the crowd. They wouldn't let me get to him. I screamed even louder, "Let me see him! Where is he?" We were greeted by the authorities and the medical examiner.

The medical examiner proceeded to tell me, "Dominique has passed away and his friends have identified him. We know it's him. I'm sorry for your loss."

I was screaming, "I want to see Dominique myself!" I lost it when they denied my request again! Everything after that was all a blur!

My heart left me and hasn't been the same since. I don't remember how I got to my mom's house. When I got there, cars were already there! I asked one child that I knew was with Dominique, "What happened to my baby? WHAT HAPPENED TO MY BABY?"

The young man just looked out in a zombie state and in disbelief his mouth could not open. He was frozen still. He had just witnessed the most horrific thing a human being could. His best friend was instantly killed right in front of him.

I remember people started coming inside the house, and my Pastor and First Lady were there. I was numb and in shock. They sat me down, and I just looked at them. My breath was taken; it was hard to breathe. They prayed over me. That hasn't changed six years later.

How do you keep living after your one and only child is murdered in broad daylight at a tourist beach with hundreds of people on a beautiful sunny Sunday? God is my best friend, my lover, my everything! He's the only reason I'm still alive today. When I wanted an easier way out, suicide crossed my mind. He kept me. When I grieved alone when people left who I thought wouldn't, He kept me. When I didn't want to live, God kept me! I will always give Him credit, and only Him! We think we have life all figured out, and then life happens.

I've experienced loss at a very young age. I lost my father at age eleven. I was with him. I remember exactly where and when it happened. I lost my eldest sister unexpectedly when she was only twenty-four years old. I lost my grandmother in January 2014. Guess who played for her celebration service with his dad by his side? Dom. We loved her dearly! She loved making Dominique his "racaroni," as she called it. She's missed terribly and never forgotten.

But I have never experienced loss on this level, and I didn't know what to do. The burden, pain, anger, misery, and the unknown of life were heavy. I didn't care anymore. I didn't want to go back to work. I couldn't dare walk in the church and not hear him play. I was depressed. For the first time in my life, I hated life and the person who took my precious son from me. I never knew what that felt like. Growing up, my mom didn't allow me and my sisters to use the word, "hate." It was like a curse word. It took years to get through that stage of hate.

I've never had a counselor or therapist in my life. I sought after God for my problems. Looking back, the problems I had were minute to losing my baby. I went to counseling but didn't feel like it was going to help. I didn't buy into the therapy at first, but I did what was recommended. As I looked at my therapist, I wondered, *"Have you endured a loss such as this?"*

I thought about my mom; she had lost my sister. So, she knew what it felt like to lose someone you loved more than life itself. My Mom is a goat! She's strong, relentless, and a God-fearing woman. I've never seen her cry except two times in my life—at her best friend's celebration of life service and Dominique's service. She was weakened at the knees. She held me like a baby during my journey. A mother's love is unconditional. I'm a great mother because of God and her. How she raised, loved, and nurtured me was passed down to Dominique.

I thought about my childhood and how my in-home caregivers loved me and took great care of me when my parents were working in the family business. This memory helped me realize I had to seek professional help and give therapy a real try. I found that my mom and I both needed help to process losing Dominique. We went to therapy together, and I have continued to go six years later. I will never stop. God, therapy, support, and family. In that order. I've learned your support may not always come from family. You appreciate the support from strangers too. The blessing is my family hasn't left my side. I thank God for my family.

I knew I had to give back the opportunity Dominique didn't have. He loved music and life so much. I was determined to keep his legacy and memory alive. WalkforDom was birthed. Both of his grandmothers love to walk. They enjoyed walking with him as well. My trainer at the time, said let's name it WalkforDom; it means something, it's natural. A nonprofit 501(c)3 raising funds to send youth to college seeking performing arts in college. In 2016, Dominique's Musician Corner Scholarship Fund was created. We have been awarded six scholarships in Dominique's memory. God gets all the glory and praise. We've had our first recipient graduate from college in May 2021.

Through my stages of grief, I started to have a purpose of living again. I learned through seeking God, fasting, prayer, the Holy Spirit, and discernment that I couldn't do this journey alone. Dominique transitioned at the age of seventeen. Yes, you heard me. He was seventeen. God used me to help others. It took years for me to see the vision, and he's still working through me. It's scary.

I will forever continue to give back to the youth. God gave me a vision, and I wasn't always obedient. We want to do things our way. I had to get out of my way and still learn to allow God to do His work. I want to transition empty! I want to complete what God has for me on the earthly rem. He restored love from hate. I'm not perfect. He gave me a reason to live again, smile, and continue to serve people. I love helping people.

Through my journey, I experienced loneliness, rediscovering myself, and finding the new Permetha. You will never get used to or get over the loss of your child. In my opinion, you learn to cope with it. Everyone's detour will look different. You will lose people along the way. That's okay; it's part of the process. You will learn to trust God and only Him.

Your perspective will change in life. You will be unbothered naturally. You will tolerate less; mental health and self-care will be a priority. You will not waste your time or allow anyone to waste yours. You will no longer take anyone for granted. You will say, "I love you," more, give flowers to those you love and care about, serve more, spend more time, travel more, and most importantly, draw even closer to God.

Surrendering to Him is not easy. Laying at His feet wasn't either. But God! Not a day goes by that I don't say the Twenty-Third Psalm. I'm excited about God and what He continues to do despite my great loss. God loves me.

I began to write and journal to get an understanding of my feelings. I needed to get them out. It helped me tremendously. I loved to color as a child and write in cursive. Writing down how I felt, especially with hate emotions and anger of my experience, was so important. Journaling became a habit more and more. My therapist said, "Write a letter to whoever it is you're talking to." That tactic worked in more ways than one. It gave me comfort, emotional release, and started the journey to forgiveness. It was not easy, wasn't easy at all. God is still working on me. Triggers and soul ties are a real thing.

Everyone's timing on healing and forgiving is different—and it is a process. It took me years to begin the process of healing—after four years of Dom's passing, I finally started my healing process. I didn't want to hate anyone during my entire life of living. I realized I was giving power to the devil. He had already taken my baby. So, I said, "I must live to operate WalkforDom and help the youth." God is my keeper!

God gave me the vision of greeting cards to comfort other parents in their time of need because I had experienced different people expressing undesired emotions as they attempted to say words of condolences. For example, when someone would say, "I know how

163

you feel," or "At least he didn't suffer long," I looked at them in horror, shocked at their choice of words. I quickly told them, "You don't say that to someone who has just lost a child." Those types of interactions were fuel for me to start my own greeting card line, so the words people shared with those who were grieving would be comforting and healing, not offensive. *What am I going to name it God? Tell me, help me.* My support group leader helped from Charlotte, NC. She even got her husband involved. They got creative and researched a meaningful word.

InDOMitable Love was born. It's filled with faith, experience, hope, comfort, and love. You feel the love when you read the inspirational verses and quotes. In addition, I was mentored by two young ladies who were already authors. How dope is that! That's why when it's your season and time, no man can hinder what God has for you. I thank God for covering me daily and keeping me. Without Him, I cannot do anything. He gets all the praises and glory!

InDOMitable Love is special to me. It's my love story about Dominique and me. Motherhood has changed my life, and I miss it dearly. This story is a piece of my journey and the unconditional love I have for my son—the beloved Dominique Xavier-Milton Williams. God has angels placed all around me daily so I can feel comforted as I pursue my calling.

Dom, your legacy will live on forever, and your spirit is real. You're my angel. I miss you and love you.

PROMISE, PURPOSE, AND PAGEANTS

DONNA S MURRELL

Waking up from a nightmare of an aneurysm that I never knew I had was unimaginable. I was going about my everyday activities of being a wife, mother, and daughter, and continuing to work a job I have had for more than twenty-five years. On my way home from work, I was suddenly hit from behind by a company truck. The next day, I went to work as usual. While at work, I began to feel very dizzy. My co-workers called my husband, and he immediately took me to the hospital. I began to feel an intense, agonizing pain in the back of my head. It was like nothing I had ever experienced before.

After arriving at the hospital, they immediately sent me for an MRI and a cat scan. I was feeling nervous and scared. I was wondering what was going on. After waiting for hours for the results, the doctor told my husband and me that they had found an aneurysm in my brain. When an aneurysm ruptures, it results in bleeding in the space between the brain and surrounding tissue. In most cases, the blood can block the circulation of the fluid surrounding the brain and spinal cord. Immediately, I was scheduled for surgery, which lasted for six hours. Knowing people who have not survived such a discovery reminded me of instances in my family that were devastating.

Let me share some highlights of my life and the reasons for praying every day. At the age of eighteen, my dreams were to become a fashion runway model. I did not want to go to college like everyone else. I saw nothing wrong with college, but it was just not for me. After discussing my decision with my parents about modeling and wanting to attend Barbizon School of Modeling and Acting, they were so supportive.

This is when my career really began for me. I started modeling for major department stores in fashion shows and traveling. After graduating from modeling school, I became a part-time modeling and acting instructor. I decided to recruit models for my own Modeling Troupe and produce fashion shows. That was not enough, so I opened my own modeling agency business–Montezic Model Management. I was loving my life.

In 1983, when I was twenty-four years old, I became a mom, giving birth to an adorable baby boy named Montez. I didn't know if I was ready for that, but it was a true blessing knowing that my life was about to change. Not long after giving birth, I married **Brian**, my child's father. He had just returned from being in the military. I began to enjoy married life. He was a hardworking and wonderful husband. It started as a life of happiness, but after five years of marriage, things began to change drastically.

In 1988, I had my second child—another adorable baby boy we named Armani. I couldn't believe it. I had two children. Another true blessing from God. I knew I was young, but being a mom was teaching me about strengths and dealing with fears I didn't know I had. My husband began to change. It was not domestic violence. I saw changes in his behavior. He no longer talked to me. He stayed away from home more. Of course, the first thing that comes to mind was...is he having an affair? At the time, we had only one car. I would wait for him to pick me up from work. I would wait and wait and wait. Sometimes, he never showed up. I was so embarrassed to call anyone to pick me up.

Brian began to receive phone calls during the middle of the night. The calls became threatening. I asked him what was going on. I found out he was using drugs. We began to receive threats because he owed someone money. Some days, I would look out the window and see men sitting in a car outside our home. I did not want my children to get caught up in this, because they were my world. I was petrified.

Although Brian was a good husband who let drugs take control and ruin what we had as a family, I could no longer live like this. I told my parents about my situation. They were relieved I wanted to come home. So, knowing my husband would be gone for a few days, I packed our things and left without letting him know anything. I filed for divorce and moved to a new house to begin a better life for me and my boys.

My sister Gayle, my brother in-law, and her three children had come home for the weekend to visit our mom to celebrate Mother's Day. They lived in Georgia, and it had been a while since they had come to Charlotte. So, I could not wait to see them. She was my oldest sister, and we talked on the phone almost every single day. We had a bond like best friends. It was such a beautiful sunny day in May. We had plans for all the family to come over.

They finally arrived late on a Friday night. I ran to the top of the driveway as soon as they pulled up. Oh, my goodness. If you could see the smiles on our faces. We embraced one another for so long I didn't think either of us would let go. My little nieces and nephew got out of the car running towards me with big hugs. We walked towards the house where the rest of the family was waiting. She hadn't seen her nephew Montez in a while. He was three years old at the time. She was so glad to see him because he had grown so much.

Waking up early Saturday morning, my sister wanted to go to the mall. On our way to the mall, we talked and laughed about everything. It was nothing like spending time together. While at the mall, she was so happy. She saw friends she hadn't seen since high school and friends she grew up with from our neighborhood. After a few hours at the mall, we decided to go back home before Mom got on us because Gayle had come home to spend time with her.

This was one of the best days ever! Everyone finally showed up— our family, including cousins, nieces, nephews, and some of our neighbors. My mom was so happy. All the children and grandchildren together. We loved getting together. We talked, laughed, danced, played games, and had a ball.

We knew my sister Gayle and her family would be leaving to go back to Georgia soon. We wanted to spend as much time together as possible. Sundays has always been very special for our family, still today. Our parents prepared Sunday Dinner. This one was a special Mother's Day Sunday Dinner. My parents had prepared ham, potato salad, baked chicken, rice and gravy, green beans, and mom's rewarding sweet potato pie. Everything was so delicious. Shortly after eating, I could not believe it was time for my sister to leave. It seemed as if she had just gotten here. But I understood, she had to return to her home.

A few hours later, the phone rang. All I can remember is receiving a phone call that no one ever wants to receive. I will never forget hearing these words, "Your sister has been in a car accident, and she didn't make it. I'm sorry, but she died."

I immediately dropped the phone, ran out of the house screaming and crying to the top of my lungs, "Lord, no, no, no—not my sister." I could not believe what I was hearing. She was just with me.

After composing myself the best I could, I asked, "How are my nieces and nephew?"

"They are all in the hospital with injuries."

I couldn't believe it. How will they endure losing their mom? I remember her saying to me, "I put gas in your car," followed by us laughing together. I watched her slowly drive away with her husband and three children heading back to Georgia. Never thought those would be the last words I would hear from her. How? Why God? It was Mother's Day. A day that we celebrate the woman who gives life. This was a day that our mom would never want to relive. All I could think about was my mom and my sister's three children, my nieces, and nephew.

Our next-door neighbor who was a nurse came over to check on me regularly due to the state I was in. After finally coming out of what I thought was a nightmare, I just wanted to be with my mom. I knew she was shocked, hurt, and devastated. Her first-born child was gone. Was this really happening? Her husband survived the accident, not receiving any injuries. You read and hear about situations like this, but you never think it will happen to your family. How will I explain to my three-year-old son that his Auntie is gone? He was just getting to know her.

God, I never knew that my heart could endure so much pain and heartache. I needed to be there for my nieces and nephew who were still hospitalized and unaware of the loss of their mother. Most importantly, my mother needed me. Her first-born child had died on Mother's Day at the young age of twenty-nine.

Approximately seven years after the death of my oldest sister, my sister, Renee, suddenly became very ill. She was not eating, not sleeping, and was having severe headaches. We took her to be evaluated by medical doctors. She was given various tests to determine what was wrong. Later, we were told that she had a rare medical diagnosis related to her brain, which would eventually affect her internal organs. They gave her six months to live.

After my parents' oldest child died in a car accident, and now Renee is given this horrendous diagnosis and told she does not have much longer to live, how will my parents accept this? I was not accepting it. My family was not accepting it. We are a family of faith. Faith is trust and confidence in God. Faith is the substance or assurance of things we hope for but have not yet received. Faith comes before a prayer is even answered. And that is what we have within us.

Fifteen years later, we still continue to do what is needed to care for my sister to keep her comfortable. Year after year, things get harder. I often visit to help my parents. So thankful to have Miss G, my sister's CNA, assisting my parents with Renee's daily care.

One day our Aunt Vivian Roberts began bringing angels to Renee. It was the beginning of something so beautiful. Every time someone visits her, they would bring an angel. My dad had to build shelves to put them on. They are all over her dresser—big, small, porcelain, glass, all types. Her bedroom looks like a sanctuary of more than 250 angels watching over her. The Charlotte Observer heard about Renee's angels and did a beautiful story on her. We know these angels are watching over her and our family each day. We did not give up, because we know who our God is.

More than twenty years have passed, and Renee is still alive. Her days may consist of looking at soap operas, watching movies, sitting on the front porch with a smile on her face, but she never complains. Even though she is not leaving the house unless she has a doctor's appointment, my mom makes sure Renee is dressed nicely every day. If she is feeling up to it, we take her for rides. She makes sure she has on her jewelry and angel pins.

I think of Renee throughout my day, how suddenly her life changed. How suddenly our lives changed. No warnings. No signs. Just life happening. My sister, who is a mother and grandmother, for her, it is hard. Not being able to do the things that others do. I try to put a smile on her face as much as I can. Being a faith-driven family, my sister is a true miracle of what God can do, because it is not over until God says it over. I thank God daily for letting me still love on my sister.

Being raised in a fun-loving, churchgoing, respected family, I am forever grateful. My parents moved into their home and still live there today, sixty-one years later. I remember going on vacation to the beach, to the mountains, and my dad taking us to the county fair. I can truly say I have lived a blessed life.

Your life takes you through ups and downs, hills and valleys. Sometimes you keep a smile on your face, even though you are hurting deep inside. Other days you may cry while listening to your favorite gospel songs. Trying to be a strong caring mom, a loving wife, and working a full-time job, can be challenging. At the same time while growing a small business, I want to make a difference for girls who may need a role model or mentor in their life.

I finally received my angel, my daughter, Diamen. Thankful for our wonderful, ambitious, and talented grown children—Montez, Armani, and Diamen. Nothing fills my heart more than being a mom, until you become a G-Ma. That is what I am to my beautiful, smart granddaughter, Phoenix, daughter of my oldest son, Montez. This little angel has changed my world. The passion of pageantry and her love of wanting to be a part of it, really makes the difference. When I hear her say, "G-Ma let's do a pageant," it warms my heart knowing how special this is to me and her.

After being single for ten years, I was finally blessed to marry the man of my dreams, Eugene E. Murrell, Sr. I never thought I would get married again. Never say never. I'm thankful to have such a wonderful, supportive, loving, and god-fearing husband. He is the father that my children have always needed.

I have thought so many times of wanting to give up on my business and my passion. I was not receiving the support from others like I thought I would. As I continue to pursue my passion of directing pageants and coaching girls, my husband continues to push, motivate, and encourage me. I decided not to give up.

My best friend, Nichelle Nelson, has always been there for me, no matter what. I am so thankful to have her in my life. We have had the opportunity to share so much. Triumphs. Tragedies. Births. Celebrations. Ups and downs. Being a professional model, she moved away for a few years to New York, where she pursued her dream as an Editor of a Fashion Magazine. Although we lost touch for a little while, we never lost love. I was so glad she decided to come back to Charlotte. When she did, my life changed.

With Nichelle by my side, my businesses began to take off. She knows my business savvy and style. Nichelle became the Assistant Director of my modeling agency and Assistant Director of Carolina Girls Rock Pageant LLC. Friends forever and Sisters for life! I am forever grateful to have Nichelle as "My Bestie."

Our family grew up in church. Our mom always says to us, "Keep God first in your life," and "always trust in him." My wisdom was not in the wisdom of man, but in the power of God. I never thought about my parents, now eighty-seven years old, having to care for their child, who is now sixty-three. Normally the roles are reversed, but we don't know what tomorrow holds. Each day we are praying that she will get better, but nothing changes. But she is still here and in no pain.

My parents' lives were suddenly put on hold. Plans they had made to travel when they retired. Stopped. Plans to do nothing but rest. Changed. With my sister in a wheelchair, unable to walk or care for herself, her being anywhere else other than in the home where she grew up, never crossed my parents' minds. They did not listen when some people suggested they put Renee in a facility. They made a vow that as their child, no matter how old Renee is, they will take care of her as long as they are able.

Years ago, when I was asked to judge a beauty pageant, I was so excited. With my years in modeling, I knew it would be a positive transition. I traveled and judged pageants all over the United States, but I did not see what I wanted to see. Beauty queens had grace, poise, and confidence. I decided, I was going to start my own pageant organization and create what I want to see on stage. So, I started Carolina Girls Rock Pageant LLC in 2016.

As I took this bold step towards making my dream come true, questions and concerns crossed my mind. *How can I start a pageant business? My parents need me to help with my sister. I just had brain surgery a year ago.* I was reminded that God spared my life for a reason, and He has a greater purpose for me. So, I made a promise to God that I would work hard to make my dream come to fruition.

Pageantry is based on inner beauty, as well as personality and presentation. My focus was placed on helping young girls understand the importance of gaining self-confidence, learning communication skills, learning the rules of competition, and achieving and setting personal goals for themselves.

I am who I am by the Grace of God and the faithfulness of my mom and dad. God has positioned me to be a nurturer, have compassion and empathy, and be here for my parents, my family, and my Princesses and Queens. I am loving, caring, and inspiring. All my trust is in God for me to do whatever is needed to continue to care for my sister and my parents. I am forever thankful to still have them all.

Why did it all happen? You never know why things happen in your life. I'm blessed God spared me, which empowered me to do what I do. I want to be that person people know they can count on. Girls compete. Women empower. I am that woman who will empower girls to achieve their best. Giving every girl individual attention is important to me, because all girls are created in their own way. I make sure they are confident and ready, whether as a contestant in pageantry, preparing to speak to an audience, walking gracefully on stage, or knowing how to conduct themselves in an interview. It's important I get to know my contestants and prepare them for the pageant world by giving them great advice and guidance. But it doesn't stop there. I provide them with coaching they can take into their everyday life. Being able to talk to an audience about something you feel passionate about is a major accomplishment.

Having a meaningful purpose in your life and being able to share it is so fulfilling. When you understand that your purpose is tied to your passion, everything opens up. I am a woman who wants to help others. If I can change one girl's life, I have made a difference. Carolina Girls Rock Pageant LLC and my personal coaching business is the foundation to recognizing each client's accomplishments while encouraging her to set goals for her future.

I know I have more to do. I recognize my ability and desire to create pageants and encourage girls. I am stepping into my purpose through a selfless service. This is my opportunity to glorify God and serve others in love and passion. I look to Jesus as the perfect example of someone who stepped into his purpose through selfless service. As Jesus said, "Not my will, but your will be done," (Matthews 26:39). He died so that we can step into our purpose. He died so that we can help others do the same.

Our girls are Queens in training and have much to learn and much more growing to become who they are destined to be. Nothing is more impressive than being secure in the unique way God created each of us and to see *ourselves* as God sees us. In the words of Oprah Winfrey, "Think like a Queen. A Queen is not afraid to fail. Failure is another steppingstone to greatness." God has given me a bigger purpose and I am now ready to continue my path to letting all girls know to continue to wear their invisible crown.

FINDING MY SON
JACQUELINE SINCLAIR

My son was two years old when his father took him away from me. Alvin was once the man of my dreams. But once he found out I was pregnant, things weren't the same, and we broke up shortly after that. I had the baby when I was twenty-one. As a single mom, it was not easy, and I knew I needed to build a better life for myself and the baby.

An opportunity came for me to go into a training program to further my career, but the opportunity was in another country. I loved my son, and it was painful to know that I would have to leave him so I could make a better life for both of us. I cried so many nights and beat myself up, wondering whether I was making the right decision. I decided to go for it.

It was just about time for me to deploy for training in England for nine months. I reached out to Alvin and his mother to ask for assistance with my son. I knew they would be able to help take care of him while I was away. Alvin was not happy about the news and did not want to assist me. I explained to him that I wanted to position myself to better provide for our son. Although it did not sit well with him, he agreed and reluctantly took our baby to live with him. That night, my heart felt so heavy, I cried myself to sleep.

Soon, I left Jamaica for my training. Once I got settled, I called Alvin to see how my son was doing.

"Alvin, this is Jackie."

As soon as he heard my voice, he said, "Under no circumstance will you ever be able to see or speak to my child again. When you get back, you will never get the opportunity to have any connection with him." Then, he hung up the phone. I was devastated. Why does he want to hurt me by keeping my child from me? I tried calling Alvin several more times to speak to my son, but my calls were never answered!

After I returned from my training, I went straight to Alvin's last known address. His mother answered the door.

"Honey, your son is at a boarding school, but Alvin will never let you see him. He said numerous times that as far as he is concerned, you're dead."

I was crushed! I knew he was doing this to me because his mother had left him with his aunt to better herself to support him when he was a child; and he never forgave her. Now he's holding that against me. I tried explaining to her that he's the father of my son, and there shouldn't be any problem with him taking care of his child until I returned to the island.

"I'm a good mother," I shouted. "He cannot stop me from seeing my child. This is my only child! You guys cannot do this to me." I couldn't understand his reasoning, but I was not going to stop until I saw my child.

Alvin's grandmother, Audrey, knew that I was searching for my son. One day, she called me to her home, "Jackie, I have watched you visit this house so many times. I can see the pain in your eyes. You carried that child for nine months and almost died in the process. Let me tell you something, no one can take your child away! *You* brought him into this world. I will help you, if I can."

"Thank you," I said. She clearly understood my pain and knew I loved my son. Tears trickled down my face as I turned and walked away. I felt empty, desperate, and alone. I will find my son! The hunt is on!

Grandma Audrey called me every time my son came to visit her. She would tell me what time to come by so I could see my baby boy. My heart rejoiced every chance I got to see and speak to him, even if it had to be without Alvin's knowledge. But one day, Alvin's grandmother called and sounded very sad.

"What's wrong?"

"Alvin found out that you've been coming to the house to see your son. He said he's not going to bring him to my house anymore."

I felt horrible! I had tried on many occasions to speak with Alvin about our son, but he continued to hide my own child from me. It's as if he's punishing me for leaving the island to improve my skills so I could take better care of our son. I have cried so many times and asked God, "Why me?"

A few weeks later, I found out that Alvin had left Jamaica and moved to another country. I went to Alvin's mother right away and asked, "Where is my son? Where can I find him?"

"His father took him to the states."

"Where?" I asked in disbelief.

"The United States of America."

I felt a wave of anger, fear, pain, disbelief, and hopelessness wash over me. *My son is gone from me forever*, I thought. I fell to the floor and sobbed. After I composed myself, the need to find my son gave way to a determination I never knew I had. *I will find him, whatever it takes, and however long it takes, I thought.* I knew I needed to get a visa to visit the United States. So, I immediately started making arrangements to go to the U.S. embassy.

A few days later, I had an interview at the United States Embassy in Jamaica. Afterward, they told me I failed the interview. I was devastated. But the burning desire to find my son kept me encouraged. So, I walked across the street to the Canadian Embassy. I mustered up confidence and walked in with victory on my mind. I turned in the paperwork and sat down and waited. Soon, my name was called. I couldn't believe it! I was successful! Armed with a Canadian visa, I knew I was finally going to find my boy. I whispered a prayer thanking God for favor.

When I got back home from the embassy, I broke down crying when I saw my son's clothes, his little shoes, and toys. I missed him so much. I blamed myself for this situation. Perhaps if I had stayed in Jamaica instead of going to the training, maybe I would still have him with me.

My son was the first thing I thought about when I woke up each morning, and the last thing I thought about at night. I kept hearing his voice crying out for me. My mum was worried I would have a mental breakdown. She suggested I see a doctor.

During my appointment, the doctor said, "I can treat you for a physical illness, but for the illness in your heart, that is up to you to treat it."

That night, I lay in bed thinking about the doctor's words as tears streamed down my face. I knew I couldn't go on like this. If I didn't control my emotions, I might go crazy. If I became insane, I wouldn't be able to find my child. So, from that point on, I made a conscious effort to avoid getting upset and to concentrate all my energy on finding my son.

The next day, I went to visit my friend, Tricia. "Tricia, do you know where my son is?"

"Jackie, I'm not sure where he is. I wish I did."

On November 10, 1989, I arrived in Canada. Because of the stress of moving to a new place and trying to find my son, I felt so weak and worn. So, I cried out to God, "It's me again Lord, I am coming to you with my arms open wide and with a broken heart because I need to find my child. Please tell me what to do?"

Three years slowly passed by as I continuously searched for my son in Canada, to no avail. One day, my friends told me they were going to Niagara Falls at the New York-Canadian border. I didn't have a visa to visit New York, so I prayed, "Lord, that's where my son is. I have to find him. Please make a way."

A few days later, a friend contacted me. "Jackie, you can use my travel papers if you want. Since I'm married, I have a different last name now–and I don't use those papers anymore."

"Thank you!"

The day of the trip I was holding her papers in my hand. Fear overcame me because I had never done anything like this before. However, I was willing to try to cross the border so I could find my child. I prayed for protection and a safe journey. I didn't know that God was already clearing the way for me.

We got dressed, got in the car, and started driving towards the border. About half an hour into the drive, snow started falling so heavy that we had to drive extremely slow. When we got to the checkpoint, the immigration officer didn't check our papers because of the snow blizzard. He waved us through saying, "PLEASE DRIVE CAREFULLY!"

I smiled and shouted, "God bless you."

As soon as we crossed the U.S. border, the snow stopped. I started praising God. My friends looked at me, not understanding the magnitude of my praise and how grateful I was. I thanked them for taking the risk to get me across the border. They chipped in and bought me a bus ticket to Manhattan, New York.

I got on the bus and prayed for safe travel. "Lord, you have kept me thus far. Please keep me safe and provide a place for me to stay in New York." After a long nine-hour ride, I arrived in Manhattan. My dad and sister lived in New Jersey. I was sure they would let me stay with them until I figured things out.

I called my father first. Although he was never a father to me, I was hoping he would care enough to help me now. The phone rang. "Hello, may I speak to my father?"

"Who is this?" his wife said.

"I am Dee's daughter."

"Dee's daughter? I have never heard of you," she said.

My heart was crushed. I swallowed my pride and asked again, "Can I please speak to my father?"

"He's not here, and I don't know when he will be home," she said and hung up.

So, I called my older sister, Jasmine. I explained my situation and asked if I could stay with her.

"NO! You should have made preparations *before* you came here. I have my friend visiting with me. So, I have nowhere for you to stay."

I couldn't believe she said, "No." I started to remind her of all the times I helped her before she left the island, but God stopped me. I hung up the phone and sat down on the bench in the bus station. With tears trickling down my face, I said, "Lord, you have brought me this far, please take this pain away from me." I called my friend, Emily, who lived in the city. She said she was not able to put me up that night but could accommodate me the following day. I was so relieved. But this meant I had to spend the night in the bus station.

Emily picked me up after she got off work. After a few days, I was able to find a job in New York. I tried to find information about my son, but it was futile. My mother and my son's great grandmother reminded me to keep looking for him. But I couldn't find anything on Alvin or my son. I checked other states, but only came to a dead end. I decided the only other state left was Florida. My best friend, Angela, was living there at the time. After having a conversation with her, she said I could come stay with her.

I immediately packed up and headed down to the sunny state of Florida. I found a job working for Royal Caribbean cruise line on the weekends and Nova Southeastern University during the weekdays. The income from these jobs allowed me to support myself and put some money aside.

One day, Angela and I went grocery shopping in a Caribbean grocery store. As we stood in the checkout line, I noticed a tall gentleman standing in front of me. The shape of his body reminded me of Alvin. I turned to Angela and whispered, "He looks like my son's father."

"Alvin!" I shouted! The man turned around. Sure enough, it was him! I couldn't believe I had finally found him. He looked shocked to see me. I shouted, "You kidnapper! Give my child back to me! You stole my child." It had been nine years since I had seen my son.

People started to gather around to see what was going on. Alvin dropped his groceries and rushed out of the store. I did the same. By the time I got outside, he had gone through another door but quickly came out looking upset. I couldn't believe it! *He had my son with him!* That's when I realized he had been at the barbershop next door while Alvin was in the grocery store.

I ran over to them, but Alvin blocked me from getting close to him. He held my son tightly and walked briskly towards his car.

I shouted, "Alvin Jr., I am your mother! It's me. I am your mother. Your father has been hiding you from me."

My son stopped and looked at me. Then, his father pushed him into the car.

I was frantic! I didn't want to lose my son again.

Angela yelled, "Get in the car! We are going to follow them!" Before we could take off, a car blocked us in.

"No! No! I cried. I've lost him again," I said, watching the car pull away. My heart sank—I was on an emotional roller coaster.

That night, I cried out to the Lord, "Lord, why are you allowing me to suffer? My heart is in so much pain." Then Philippians 4:6-7 came to mind, "Do not be anxious about anything, but in everything by prayer and supplication with thanksgiving let your requests be made known to God and the peace of God, which surpasses all understanding, will guard your hearts and your mind in Christ Jesus."

"But Lord, you already know my pain. Why are you giving me more pain?"

The Lord whispered, *"My grace is sufficient for you, for my power is made perfect in your weakness."*

At that moment, I felt God's love. He reminded me of Romans 8:18, "For I consider that the suffering of this present time is not worth comparing with the glory that is to be revealed." Now, I understood that God had it covered.

I didn't see my son again, but I knew I had planted questions in his mind the day I saw him and told him his father had taken him away from me. I still continued searching for him.

I was so glad when my friend, Tricia, came to visit me. I told her everything I had found out about Alvin and my son, even the close encounter we had. I poured my heart out to her. I told her I never understood how Alvin was always a step ahead. She hugged me and assured me everything would work out.

Months later, I found out Tricia, who I trusted and who was Alvin Jr.'s godmother, was telling Alvin everything that I told her. She was even staying at his house and sleeping with him. This whole time, I did not know she was feeding him lies about me to make him angry and resentful. I had turned to her for comfort and confided in her about all my difficulties with Alvin.

Now, it made sense—each time I tried to locate my son and told Tricia new information I had discovered, she apparently told Alvin everything. Then, he would move my son to another location before I could find them. I felt so betrayed and heartbroken.

Ten years after the incident in the grocery store, I had my own house, a good job, and was stable. One day, I was sitting at my desk at work when I heard something.

"Look up the name again!"

"Is that you, Lord?" I said. Alvin's name came to me. So, I typed it in the computer. Immediately, an address popped up. I pressed print. I ran to my friend's desk. "I found an address for my son's father!"

"How did you do that?"

My eyes filled with tears, "The Lord spoke to me."

"You've been entering his name in the computer all along and nothing happened.

"But God says it is time."

She looked at me in disbelief. "Okay, if you say so."

We put the address in Google map. We looked at each other, shocked—the address was nearby where I lived.

"I'm going to this address after work," I said.

She expressed concern for my safety, but I assured her I was ready for this challenge. I left work and drove to the address. When I got there, no one was at home, but some young boys were playing basketball near the house.

Someone asked, "Who are you looking for?"

I replied, "Alvin Jr. "Do you know him?"

"Yes, but his father doesn't allow him to come out. Anyway, he's not home.

I noticed a "For Sale" sign in front of the house. I inquired when the father would be home.

"On Sunday."

I thanked them and immediately started preparing my mind for what I needed to do next.

After church, my best friend and I went to Alvin's house. She was scared for me, but I was determined to find my son at any cost.

When we arrived, I knocked, and Alvin came to the door. I was wearing a wide-brimmed hat and spoke with a British accent. He didn't seem to recognize me. I told him I was interested in buying the house. We told him we were hoping we could look at the house. He showed us the entire house. I saw a large picture of my son on the wall and asked, "Where is your son?"

"In the army," he replied.

"Where is his mother? Did she agree for him to enlist in the army?"

"She gave him away when he was two years old."

I just wanted to jump on him and beat him. It was really hard, but I kept my composure. "Why did you allow him to go into the army?"

"He did it on his own without my knowledge."

That's when I knew in my heart that they didn't have a great father and son relationship. With the information I gathered about my son from Alvin, I was able to locate the military base that recruited him.

The following Monday, I spoke with an officer who knew Alvin Jr. I tearfully explained my situation to him. He said he would contact my son but couldn't make any promises.

Later that day, Alvin Jr. called. He told me he would be returning home soon.

A few weeks later, he knocked on my door. When I first saw him, I had an overwhelming feeling of joy, but then, anxiety swept over me. What if he didn't accept my love or accept me as his mother?

Alvin Jr. swept my fears away when he hugged me and said, "Mom, I want to get to know you and build a relationship with you, but it will take time since we've been separated for eleven years."

Through praying, talking, sharing our past, revealing our struggles and pain, we began the healing process. It could not be achieved overnight. We have talked on the telephone and met on several occasions. I told him what transpired leading up to his abduction and my life after the abduction. He shared with me about his life, the things he did, his successes, challenges, and about his relationship with his father.

Since we reunited, the deep void that existed in both of our lives has been filled. We have developed a close bond that transcends the time we were separated. We share a lot through general talk, humor, and interest in each other's lives. Our relationship keeps getting stronger over time. We have a mutual respect and love that will never be broken again through any force or action of man.

Finding my son was my dream deferred. This is my testimony! **God answers prayer!** He may not come when you call him, but He will be there on time. He is an on-time God!

GOD'S PROMISE–MY CALLING!

DONNA L THOMPSON

Life In Jamaica

As a child, I spent quite a bit of time daydreaming, drawing, writing, planning my future, and thinking about all the remarkable things I would accomplish. My life was on a schedule; everything was written down. I had to achieve all my goals within a specific time, which is how detailed I had my life planned out. I even had a timeframe for getting married, having children, completing college, and starting my own business because being an entrepreneur was my goal.

In Jamaica, there were nights I would sit on the wall that surrounded my home, gazing into the night skies, asking myself if I would ever see and experience the wonders of the world? My home was safe and secure but seemed to limit my adventurous nature and curiosity of the world. So much time had passed with me dreaming about these things that eventually, it seemed as though it was never going to happen.

Finally! The opportunity came for me and my mother to leave and travel to New York City. I could hardly wait to leave home so I could see what was beyond the stars I had been gazing upon for years. I will never forget the night before my mom and I were to leave home headed to the United States. The excitement and adrenaline pulsated throughout my entire body. Although I tried to drift off to sleep, I couldn't. The night seemed to take an eternity to end, and daylight stayed at bay as if it did not want to come. Those last few hours in Jamaica seemed to stretch out as if the island did not want to let me go, or so I thought.

It was my first time traveling on an airplane. The thought of it felt scary, yet there was something magical about it that made me feel great. As I gazed about the huge plane looking at the other passengers, I couldn't believe how many people were on the aircraft with us. There were young, middle-aged, and old people all clustered together, some smiling and laughing, others sitting quiet as they looked about. Before takeoff, I prayed we would all get to New York safely. I couldn't believe that my new adventure would be taking me to a fairy tale place I had never been before, a big city that had almost three times the population of Jamaica. It was hard to wrap my brain around that many people in one place.

Bright Lights in the Big City

When the airplane descended and cruised over New York City, it was nighttime. Looking out of the plane's window, I was amazed that the lights were brighter than any lights I had ever seen in my life. I could not believe how many tall buildings were crammed together on one huge city block. I had never seen anything like it. It really felt like a fairy tale.

The plane soon landed, and we all grabbed our belongings and exited the plane. I was so busy taking in my surroundings in the airport, that I got caught up following the wave of people walking briskly. There were faces of all nationalities, all kinds of stores with merchandise hanging in the windows, various sounds of music playing and people talking, and everything and everyone moving about so quickly. Suddenly, I stopped, frozen in my tracks. I realized I had no idea where I was going, I was just following the crowd.

189

"Donna! Where are you going?" my mother yelled. "We need to go this way," she said pointing to the exit. As my mom and I walked out of the airport, I saw a lot of people holding signs with names and numbers on them as they scanned the wave of people coming through the doors. Finally, my mom smiled and said, "Come, this way!" I looked and there was someone there holding a sign with my mom's name on it. Well that was our ride to our next destination.

I thought to myself and smiled, *All things I've dreamed about are now possible in this new place.* New York seemed to be everything I dreamed of and had imagined it would be. There were more opportunities for me to fulfill all my dreams and goals. I planned to attend college, own my own business, and become a model, which I enjoyed doing, and I loved the arts.

Now that we were in this new city, opportunities and failures presented themselves in ways I did not expect. Not long after my mother and I arrived, she knew she needed to make money in order to take care of us. So, every day she hit the pavement looking for work. At night, she came back home, tired, and weary from her relentless effort to find a job, only to return home jobless. The welcoming atmosphere we first felt from the people who lived in this apartment building, was quickly gone. I noticed that we had begun to receive some cold stares and fewer smiles from a few of the other residents.

One evening, my mother came into our apartment and said she needed to talk to me. She looked so serious; I wasn't sure what she was going to say, but I was hoping it was good news. I knew she had been out job hunting all day, and she looked tired, but I hoped she had found a job. Anyway, I sat down on the sofa next to her waiting for her to tell me the important news.

"I know you like this place, and you've made some friends, but I'm sorry we have to move and find another place to live."

"O.K.," I said, looking sadly at my mom. Of course, I did not understand, but I certainly did not ask questions, even though I was quite curious as to why we had to move and wondered where we would go? Where we lived seemed fine to me, I had friends I went to school with who lived in the same neighborhood. We would stay outside and play games late at night. It wasn't perfect, but it seemed okay to me. So, why were we leaving?

Nevertheless, within a week, my mom had found a place for us to live. So, we moved to what would become our new home. Until this day I do not know the full dynamics as to the reason we had to move so quickly.

The New Place

As I entered the tiny room, thoughts were rushing through my head. *Is my mom crazy?* I was shocked! Our new place was no bigger than a walk-in closet with two beds, a file cabinet, and bamboo window blinds that draped the glass windows from ceiling to floor. We had a very small bathroom, no bigger than a laundry or linen closet. The room was quite dark. Why did we have to leave where we were before? What could Mom be thinking? We cannot live here! I thought to myself, *Is she serious?*

How are we going to get around? We don't even have a car, and buses are nowhere near this place. We will have to walk about a mile to the closest bus station. I was not used to taking public transportation. In Jamaica, my mom had a car for us to get around. So, this was going to be a major change for me.

Then the realization hit me. All my plans and aspirations for the things I wanted to accomplish in this new country, this new city, flew out the window. *We will never get out of this place*, I thought to my-self. I never imagined the day I left the comfort of my home back in Jamaica, that this is where we would have ended up. All these thoughts went through my head. Despair flashed across my face. I wanted to cry so badly. For the first time in my life, I realized we had nothing, *absolutely nothing*. How are we going to survive? I was so disappointed and feared the worst would happen to us.

When we first arrived in our "new" place, my mom still did not have a job. But, I knew she was doing her best to support us. I could not let her know how scared I was. So, I kept my feelings to myself and refused to let my mom know what I was thinking.

After a few weeks, my mom finally got a job, and she was happy, and I was so relieved. Then she got another job. Working two jobs was not easy, but Mom was determined to do her best to take care of us and she never complained.

Great, I thought. Things will pick up quickly and we will move from this horrible place.

Little did I know my mom was barely making enough money to pay the rent. With the little money she had left, she bought food for us to eat. Mom worked seven days a week, including holidays, and had no days off. She would get up early in the morning to head to work. When I came home from school, she was already off to work her second job. So, I did not get to see her much, only two times per week, because she was always working.

Now, the cooking situation was another story. Every day, Mom would make sure there was something prepared for me to eat. I don't know how she did it since all we had was a metal table that held our two-burner hot plate stove on it. To some people, it may be just an-other piece of furniture in the tiny room that occupied way too much space. But to us, it was our lifeline, even though because of its size, it made it challenging for us to move around in our tiny, confined space.

The Greenhouse

Our new home was actually a greenhouse where plants are kept. It appeared to have been the porch on the back of the house that the owners converted into a greenhouse but later decided to rent it. The gray filing cabinet became our closet. Our refrigerator was so small it could only hold a few items. So, we didn't have a lot of groceries. But I remember we often had chicken gizzards. It was the main meal my mother cooked. Yuck! I hate those things now, but back then, it was what my mom could afford to buy for us to eat.

There were no outlets or lights in the greenhouse. The property owner ran an extension cord from inside his house to the greenhouse so we could have electricity. As a result, everything that needed power was plugged into that extension cord. We had a television someone had given to us. It barely worked, so we had to rig it with a metal clothes hanger to get reception. I didn't care as long as we could watch something on TV.

Life in the greenhouse was so hard. We lived there for several years. My mom worked her fingers to the bones just to keep a roof over our heads and to be able to pay the bills. Grocery shopping was extremely difficult because we had to walk miles to the store and then, back home carrying the heavy grocery bags. You see, after my mom paid for groceries, she could not afford to take a taxicab, so we walked, stopped to rest, walked, and stopped to rest some more until we made it home.

No one knew where we lived or how we lived. The inside of our home was so tiny, it was barely big enough for me and my mom to move around. Having friends over was not possible because there was no room for guests! Outside, the backyard had overgrown shrubs, weeds, broken-down cars left to rot, and quick-growing kudzu vines that took over everything in the backyard, like it was the Amazon Forest. So, we led very lonely lives. All we had was each other.

When my mom was working her two jobs, I was lonely. This led me to eventually start spending more time in the streets when my mom was not home. This was the only way I could have friends and hang out with anyone, because of course, they could not come to the greenhouse. It was too embarrassing and shameful to let anyone know we were living this way.

Winters were especially brutal for us living in the greenhouse. I recall the winter of 1986 when we had a terrible blizzard. We were snowed in and could not get out of the greenhouse because the snow was packed high up against the door that led outside, and it even covered the windows. The property owner had stapled sheets of plastic around the windows during the winter months to help keep us warm. Nothing seemed to help ward of the brutal cold and chill of the elements of that winter. Days had gone by, and we were not able to get outside because the door would not open. I could tell Mom was very concerned and frustrated because she was not able to go to work, which meant she did not earn an income for that period of time. Of course, this was very challenging for her because she fought so hard to try and keep things together for us.

The Turning Point

I will never forget, one evening my mom was home, and she was cooking us something to eat. I was watching television. We heard crackling sounds but did not know where it was coming from, nor did we think anything of it. Suddenly, our tiny room started to fill with smoke. Before we knew it, a fire broke out. The extension cord that supplied us with electricity had caught on fire where it dangled over the filing cabinet that had all our clothes and other items in it.

"OMG!" I screamed, "Mom! Fire! I'm so scared! Are we going to be burned to death in this greenhouse? We can't get out the door! It won't open! I don't want to die here!"

"No!" my mom said, "I won't let that happen!" She quickly jumped into action and started putting the fire out with her bare hands. I looked at her in awe as she battled the flames that threatened to consume us. Remarkably, she was able to put out the fire without getting burned. Afterwards, she sat down and looked around our tiny room, assessing the damage. She took a few deep breaths and shook her head.

"We'll be okay," she said.

I can only imagine how terrified she must have been, knowing both of our lives were at risk. But God was on our side and helped her to be brave so she could save us that day. I was so proud of her.

I am not certain if that is when she decided we had to move, but eventually, she was able to move us out of that little greenhouse. During the years after that, life was still challenging and had many difficulties, but with each obstacle God was still blessing us and carried us through.

Dreams Died

I did not realize how much I had changed over the past few years. After living in the greenhouse, the majority of my life thereafter was spent surviving and knowing how to survive in a jungle. I lost all my dreams and aspirations for the things I wanted to accomplish. Frankly, I had forgotten about them. Life was like a blurred moment of mere existence. Even though things had changed, and life had become better, I was not able to grasp the things I once desired for myself. I became a different person, but I did not realize it at the time.

Through deferred dreams, God's calling became more evident in my life. He did not bless me to become what *I* had desired and once saw for myself. God did not bless me with the materialistic things I desired at the time. I would not have known what to do with them anyway.

God's promise and calling on my life was bigger and bolder than I could have ever possibly imagined. He removed me from the comfort of my home in Jamaica, took me to a foreign land with my mother, and placed me amongst strangers. He even made me live in a tiny greenhouse for years, as well as in other places. He was breaking me, molding me, and building me back up into the person He called me to be.

Even through the trials and tribulations, God has always carried me in the palm of his hands. He put me into the fires and carried me through the storms. It took years of trying to do things my way until I got to the point where I finally let go and gave all my concerns and worries to God, because everything I tried was not working. I could not see what he had in store for me, so he snatched me up off the path I was on, made me sit and wait for a while as he was making the way for improved things to come. At times, it was frightening and scary. Yes, I did become scared many times.

You see, while the Lord had me waiting, the Devil was also creating havoc on the home front. But all I needed to do was have faith and know that his promise would prove to be the calling he had on my life. Even though my dreams may not have manifested within the time I wanted it to or how I wanted it to, it all happened the way God intended it to all happen.

Now, when I look at my image in the mirror, I can truly say God has abundantly blessed me beyond my wildest imagination. What might have taken me a lifetime to figure out on my own, he did in a matter of months. During the Covid-19 pandemic, the Lord blessed me in ways I could not have ever imagined, nor did I see it coming. In 2021, I became an International best-selling author. I also launched my business, DBL & DLT Creations LLC, where we create authentic clothing and apparel inspired by my son, Daniel Laird, with his creativity and artwork.

In all things I do, I give God the glory. He has carried me through the storms and has blessed me with a loving and grateful heart. I will always sing praises unto the Lord and rest in his word knowing that he cares for me and never leaves me.

"The Lord is my light and my salvation-whom shall, I fear? The Lord is the stronghold of my life-of whom shall I be afraid? (Psalm 27:1)

I dedicate my chapter to my mother Barbara Phillips (Dunn).

AFFIRMATIONS

I am strong

I am confident

I am resourceful

I am purified by the fire of the Holy Spirit

I am a shining light for all to see God's good works in me

Write your personal affirmation/s here:

ABOUT THE AUTHORS

ANGELA M MITCHELL

Angela M Mitchell AKA "The Mindset Maven" is The Daughter of The Most High, a mother, grandmother, sister, and friend. She is also a mental health advocate, author, speaker, master life coach, and the founder and CEO of Back to Her.

After having experienced her own challenges with mental health disorders such as anxiety and depression that left her out of alignment with God's Purpose, she transformed her mind and changed the narrative her life story. She then decided to use her experiences to educate and advocate for other women who may be fighting similar battles.

Angela is dedicated to removing mindset barriers through both personal and professional development programs that empower women to acknowledge the limited beliefs that are holding them back, embrace and heal their Divine Feminine Energy, so that become the highest most truthful expression of themselves.

Connect with her:

angelammitchell@back2her.org

https://www.facebook.com/groups/backtoher

https://www.facebook.com/Back2Her

NADIA MONSANO

Nadia Monsano is an international bestselling author, marketing and branding specialist and a retired veteran staff sergeant after serving 10yr in the US Army. While in the military Nadia served one tour in Iraq and earned the Iraqi Freedom Medal of Honor. After retiring from the Army Nadia started working in corporate America in the medical field as a Program Director.

Nadia started her own company My Sister Keeper in February 2020. My Sister Keeper is a branding and marketing agency that offers graphic designs. Nadia has worked with women all over the United States and Internationally to help them launch their business and show up online professionally.

Connect with her at sistermykeeper@gmail.com

https://www.facebook.com/mysisterkeeper

TRINA SAN

Trina San has an Associate Degree in Health Information Technology and a Bachelor's Degree in psychology and Christian Counseling. When she is not writing, she enjoys volunteering at the Second Harvest Food Bank and Novant Health Hospice giving gardens. In her leisure time she enjoys spending time with her blended family, including their dog Lucy. Trina and her Husband Vernon lives in NC.

Connect with her at stroudtrina@gmail.com

https://www.facebook.com/trinastroudboyton

TAMIKA MCTIER

Tamika McTier is a wife, mother, speaker and entrepreneur who has broken cycles and lives without barriers. She knows firsthand that when you don't give up on yourself, anything is possible. After becoming a teen mom, statistics counted her out, but she realized that she was still the narrator of her story and could change the narrative. That empowered her to push forward and achieve every goal that she set for herself - including starting her own business, Ageless Conversations LLC. Now Tamika is on a mission to help other high-achieving married women to move beyond their perceived limitations. Armed with a powerful testimony and her signature T.A.L.K. method, Tamika equips and empowers other women to write their own stories, create their own paths, and be unstoppable in the pursuit of their dreams

Connect with her at mctier1@icloud.com

https://www.facebook.com/tamikamctier

ALLISON G DANIELS

Minister Allison G. Daniels is an International Bestselling Author who has written over 31 books, Co-Author of 14 books, Visionary Author of the book "Empowered to Win" 3rd Edition Book Anthology. She is a 2X Podcast Radio Host of Authors Chat with Allison and The Authors Lab. She is an Empowerment Speaker, Licensed Minister, Book Writing Coach and CEO/Founder of AGD Publishing Services, LLC where their mission is to turn writers into successful published authors. She has a Segment on Facebook Live @ 5am and Segment on Gospel Time Machine at 6am. She has been married to her husband Earl for over 20 years and she is the proud mother of two Queens Kristian and Damona. She is the creator of the 30 Day Write 2 Finish Book Writing Program.

Connect with her at www.allisongdaniels.com

allisongdaniels@verizon.net

https://www.facebook.com/allisongdaniels

SHANIA ELLIOTT-MCDOWELL

Shania Elliott-McDowell is a wife and a mother of four, born and raised in Brooklyn, NY. She now lives in Charlotte, N.C. She proudly served for two years in The United States Army and eight years in The National Guard. Shania has attended Johnson & Wales University, where she got her Associates in Culinary Arts. She has also received her Associates in Nursing and LPN license at Kaplan University. She is the proud owner and chef of Decadent Chefs, where she creates innovative recipes flavored with fruit. Shania is the founder of the nonprofit organization called Happiness Is Vibrant. Shania is a three-time best-selling author and an international best-selling author. She is currently working on her cookbook. Her hobbies are being a mom, reading, writing poetry, and creating new dishes. Her favorite the quote is by Janelle Monae (Embrace what makes you unique even if it makes others uncomfortable)

Connect with Shania at

www.decadentchefs.com/

shania@decadentchefs.com

CHARLES G KEARSE

Charles G. Kearse has inspired and connected audiences with his keynote presentations and workshops and his universal message about winning in life, leadership, and entrepreneurship. Charles serves as Nehemiah Project International, Director of Urban Impact Vision. For more than 30 years, he has connected companies with community organizations achieving the shared goals of doing good while turning a profit. Charles has planted four life-changing churches, started several successful businesses and created the inner-city transformation process "Pathways to Victory." Charles is a U.S Army Veteran and has a passion for connecting returning citizens to the community to build successful business models that help to transform urban communities. Charles is passionate about coaching youth and the formerly incarcerated to achieve success and significance.

Connect with Charles at charles@nehemiahproject.org

https://www.facebook.com/charleskearse

VERN HAMIL

Vern Hamil is a Jamaican born author whose goal is to be renowned in the literary world. She wants her writings to covey and message hope and inspiration for readers and, in so doing, reach a broad audience.

She has an AS in Business Management and a BS in Business Administrations. She is a mother and grandmother and loves to read, write, and cook. She currently resides in Bronx, New York, with her family.

Connect with her at vernhamil@aol.com

https://www.facebook.com/vernahamilton

TONYA BARBEE

Tonya Barbee has served in the educational field all of her adult life. She earned her M.B.A. at National-Louis University in Chicago, IL and has been working for the government in the project management field for over 35 years. Tonya is the founder of I am Still a Rose, LLC where she inspires and empowers others through coaching, speaking engagements, apparel and other products for both men and women.

She is a member of Toastmasters, "Go Pro," and has an engaging masterclass, "Be the Rose, Not the Thorn," where she teaches how to move beyond the pain after hardships to be the most beautiful rose, inside and out. Tonya is also an active member of the Eta Phi Beta Sorority, Epsilon Zeta Chapter.

She's a native of Durham, NC with four children, eight grandchildren. Her website is www.tonyabarbee.com

https://www.facebook.com/tonyabarbee

TAMRA T BUSH

Tamra T Bush has over two decades in the financial industry. She holds numerous credentials including a bachelor's degree in Business Administration (with a focus in Finance and Project Management), from AIU, and is a certified paralegal (Canisius College) and licensed insurance agent. She is an international, two-time best-selling author.

Tamra has invested her life in attaining the expertise needed to assist others to become equipped in being productive members of the community. She shares success principles that help uplift individuals so they can continue to build upon and improve their financial situation. Tamra is praised not only for her knowledge and wisdom but for her commitment to education, and passion about helping others. She is also esteemed for leading by example, having overcome her own struggles to reach out to empower others to achieve their dreams.

To connect with Tamra, visit her website at

http://www.tamratbush.com/

E-mail: info@source1associates.com

PATTY LAUTERJUNG

Patty Lauterjung is a Creative Solutions Strategist as a copy editor, writing coach, author, and speaker. She has over twenty-five years of experience capturing the voice of others and turning their written words into bestselling books, dynamic websites, engaging marketing material, college application essays, and online training programs. Her passion, priority, and purpose are to bring out the best in every client. Patty has a Bachelor of Arts in Business Management and is the owner of PL Creative Editing LLC in Charlotte, NC.

Although most people find editing boring, Patty says, "I have one of the best jobs in the world! My clients are fascinating, creative, and unique individuals. I bring my depth of knowledge, a broad range of editing experience, and commitment to exceed my clients' expectations to help them reach their audience in meaningful, engaging, and influential ways."

You can reach Patty at:

www.plcreativediting.com

plenterprises7@gmail.com

https://www.facebook.com/plcreativeediting

AMY HAYES

Amy Michelle Hayes is a Minister, Singer, Author, Ambassador, Prayer Warrior, and Intercessor. She holds a certification of Cancer Leadership and is a certified Notary Public.

She is the owner and founder of, Ames Heart of Love. AHOL is a nonprofit organization designed to spread and show love to, "ALL" people across the world. With showing love, she inspires others to forgive and love others as Jesus loves us. AHOL, feeds and clothes the less fortunate in the community. Amy also has a nursing home ministry and visit the sick with prayer and communion. She loves serving others and there is a special place in her heart for the elderly.

Connect with Amy at ahayesm@gmail.com

http://www.facebook.com/amymichellehayes

PERMETHA RUDY MILTON

Permetha "Rudy" Milton, is the Founder/CEO of Walk for Dom and InDOMitable Love Greeting Cards. When her only child, Dominique Williams, passed away at age 17 due to senseless gun violence, Rudy's life was forever changed. She used her life-changing moment to preserve her son's memory and give back to other youths so they would have the chance to lead positive, rewarding lives. Shortly after her son's death, Rudy founded Walk For Dom, a non-profit organization to raise awareness about gun violence and the need for better gun control laws. The annual walk also generates funds for Dominique's Musician Corner Scholarship. Rudy also created the InDOMitable Love Greeting Card line. Rudy is a heartfelt speaker, a genuine supporter to other parents who have lost a child to violence, and a woman seeking to fulfill God's indomitable purpose for her life.

Connect with her at info@indomitablelove.net

https://www.facebook.com/rudymilton

DONNA S MURRELL

Donna S Murrell is a Wife, Mom of 3, G-ma, the CEO/Founder of Carolina Girls Rock Pageant LLC (CGRP) and Donna Murrell Pageant Coaching. Her dream was to become a professional runway model; a dream which she accomplished and made an impact. She has been an employee with the City of Charlotte for 31 years.

With years of experience in the fashion, event planning, and pageantry world, making a first impression is of upmost importance. She has worked with several celebrities, renowned artist, national brand businesses and entrepreneurs plus appearing in major magazine and newspaper articles. Her passion, dreams and faith are the driving force behind everything she does, and her passionate response is reflected in her love for others and making a difference with girls.

Donna can be reached at dmurrellcoaching@gmail.com

or 704-904-9485

JACQUELINE SINCLAIR

Jacqueline Bonner Sinclair proudly served Jamaica Defense Force (JDF) for 10 years.

As a creative being, Jacqueline completed her studies at Saunders Culinary School where she learned the art of food presentation. She also attended Nova Southeastern University where she obtained her bachelor's degree in Business Administration with a minor in Public Speaking. She is the founder of Touch and Restored, a non-profit, based in Tamarac, Florida with a focus on battered women and abused children.

Her upcoming book The Child's Cry will be released later in 2022. Her hobbies are cooking, creative event planning, and mentoring the younger generations. Jacqueline's goal is to always encourage individuals to be the best they can be and to embrace the simple things in life.

As a wife, mother of two with 3 bonus children, Jacqueline and her husband resides in sunny South Florida.

Connect with her at jacquelinesin64@gmail.com

https://www.facebook.com/jacquelinebonner

DONNA L THOMPSON

Donna L Thompson is an International best-selling author. is a Clinical Informatics Specialists who enjoys teaching and coaching individuals to attain their full potential. Donna is a member of the Paleontology Association of Georgia and The Georgia Lupus Foundation. She is a Consultant for A&J General Contractor Inc, a Mom-preneur and Co-founder of DBL&DLT Creations founded in 2019. Donna is an International best-selling author.

Donna's passion is serving humanity, while helping others discover their natural gifts, strengths, and talents they've been blessed with and use them to become the best version of themselves.

Connect with Donna at dlthompson2009@gmail.com

https://www.facebook.com/dlthompson